Social Media and the Post-Truth World Order

"If the post-truth order is primarily marked by a generalized loss of trust in traditional sources of authority and information as well as a growing fragmentation of the media sphere, this book convincingly argues that the truth of the post-truth condition is not to be found in the details but within a global discursive space where state and non-state actors, established powers and emerging political networks, build surprising alliances to hegemonize the public sphere and upend the post-1989 world order."

—Marco Deseriis, *Assistant Professor, Scuola Normale Superiore Florence, Italy*

"Finally, we have a theory of post-truth that emerges from an international or global analysis. In this excellent development of empirically-grounded post-truth theory, Cosentino moves from well-known cases such as Pizzagate and Russian trolls in the U.S. 2016 presidential election, to cases that have received little to no attention in media and political communication studies, such as the "White Helmets" rumors amplified by Russian media in the Syrian civil war, the Facebook hate speech campaign against the Rohingya Muslim minority in Myanmar, and the disinformation apparatus that propelled Bolsonaro to power in Brazil. Cosentino's analysis is also unique in its attention to the use of an array of platforms and spaces of media that are exploited for disinformative and misinformative purposes, including 4chan and 8chan, Whatsapp, Facebook, Twitter, in addition to traditional news media. His work engages with the problems of international political economy in the post-truth matrix, especially how the agents of post-truth exploit the weaknesses of media laws. Finally, he does not shy away from drawing lessons from his case studies for technical, educational, regulatory and political intervention. *Social Media and the Post-Truth World Order* is a welcome contribution to a growing body of theory and empirical analysis in post-truth studies."

—Jayson Harsin, *Associate Professor and Chair, Global Communications Department, The American University of Paris, France*

"In this book, Gabriele Cosentino masterfully addresses perhaps the greatest lacuna in post-truth studies by demonstrating its global nature. By dedicating a substantial portion of the text to cases beyond the West, he manages to not only broaden our geographical scope of understanding post-truth but also to tease out the latter's preconditions and characteristics that remain constant across national, political, and cultural contexts and can, therefore, be seen as the phenomenon's core traits. Ultimately, this timely book demonstrates that post-truth is not some isolated manifestation of fakery, but a collective domain that spans the world as an alternative self-sustaining universe. The result is a must-read book that lays bare the emergent post-truth world order."

—Ignas Kalpokas, *Senior Lecturer, Department of Public Communication, Vytautas Magnus University, Lithuania*

Gabriele Cosentino

Social Media and the Post-Truth World Order

The Global Dynamics of Disinformation

Gabriele Cosentino
Baabda, Lebanon

ISBN 978-3-030-43007-8   ISBN 978-3-030-43005-4   (eBook)
https://doi.org/10.1007/978-3-030-43005-4

Cover illustration: © John Rawsterne/patternhead.com

This Palgrave Pivot imprint is published by the registered company Springer Nature
Switzerland AG
The registered company address is: Gewerbestrasse 11, 6330 Cham, Switzerland

Acknowledgements

I would like to thank Berke Alikasifoglu for turning a class research project into the unexpected and enlightening inspiration for this book; Edwin Nasr for helping me navigate the murky waters of the on-line conversations on the Syrian Civil War; Gabriel Martin for being the most reliable and relaxing presence an academic could wish for during lunch breaks; Waddick Doyle and Ted Magder for being consistent friends and mentors during the twists and turns of my academic career; Bani Brusadin and Jorge Luis Marzo for allowing me to present part of this work at a fun and interesting conference in Barcelona; Marco Deseriis for sharing a few brilliant insights when the theory part of this book was struggling to take shape; Matteo Montaguti for showing me an exciting and unsettling perspective on the world of on-line subcultures; Oriol Andres for the numerous inspiring exchanges on Middle Eastern politics; Luigi Anzivino for demonstrating, despite the geographical distance, true and unyielding friendship; I would also like to express my gratitude to my editor at Palgrave Macmillan, Michelle Chen, for believing in this project and for supporting me throughout the writing process. I am also grateful to the three anonymous reviewers for offering me valuable and constructive criticism of my book proposal. My wife Vera was there constantly to help me through the hurdles of researching and writing, giving me courage and motivation when I needed them the most. My son Michele always reminded me that having fun should be everyone's life priority, even when working. My daughter Anna was born in Beirut a few months before the breakout of the 2019 Lebanese protests, and she brought with her the most joyous revolution one could ever wish for. This book is dedicated to the memory of James Le Mesurier, founder of the White Helmets.

CONTENTS

CHAPTER 1

The Post-truth World Order

Abstract This chapter posits the post-truth condition as a phenomenon with a global reach causing significant geopolitical effects, and it locates its discussion within the academic debate on cultural and political globalization. The epistemic crisis ushered in by postmodern relativism is discussed in the chapter as being inherently related to the trust crisis suffered by gatekeepers and truth-arbiters of twentieth-century modernity, such as mainstream media and mass parties. Changes in the political economy of media, the hybridization of entertainment and information and the rise of populist politics are also regarded as conducive to the current post-truth condition. The broader state of crisis of the Western liberal democratic model and of neoliberal market capitalism are identified as the conceptual perimeters within which post-truth acts as a catalyst of ideological tensions and geopolitical power struggles.

Keywords Post-truth · Disinformation · Misinformation · Fake news · Postmodernism · Propaganda · Populism

1.1 POST-TRUTH GOES GLOBAL

During a speech at a New York summit of the Anti-Defamation League in November 2019, the comedian Sacha Baron Cohen, known for his outrageous impersonations such as that of Borat—"the first fake news journalist in history"—for once put on a stern face and delivered a scathing

© The Author(s) 2020
G. Cosentino, *Social Media and the Post-Truth World Order*,
https://doi.org/10.1007/978-3-030-43005-4_1

attack against "the greatest propaganda machine in history" created by a handful of Internet companies that he blamed for facilitating hate and violence around the world.[1] Baron Cohen criticized the algorithms that curate the information delivered by Internet companies such as Google, Facebook and Twitter, which "deliberately amplify content that triggers outrage and fear." For the British entertainer, by giving a platform to demagogues and bigots who appeal to humans' worst instincts, by allowing conspiracy theories to be watched billion of times and to travel from the fringes to the center of public discourse, and by letting hateful speech against minorities to run rampant, social media companies are upending the very democratic order of our societies. "Democracy, which depends on shared truths, is in retreat", lamented Baron Cohen, "autocracy, which depends on shared lies, is on the march." In a blow to Facebook decision not to fact-check political advertisements and against Mark Zuckerberg's claim that the main goal of his company is to protect people's right to free speech, the comedian bitterly joked that "If Facebook were around in the 1930s, it would have allowed Hitler to post 30-second ads on his 'solution' to the 'Jewish problem'." He concluded by advocating the need for holding Internet companies responsible for their content: "It's time to finally call these companies what they really are – the largest publishers in history."

Baron Cohen's tirade against global social platforms was as timely as it was provocative, and it encapsulated many of the grievances and anxieties that over the past few years have emerged in public conversations discussing the relation between social media and politics. After years spent celebrating these technologies as empowering and liberating, the public opinion has now come to realize that when giant private companies give a platform to millions of people worldwide with the main goal of generating engagement, dire consequences can ensue. More broadly, the concerns voiced by the creator of Borat, who knows very well the power of lies and fabrications having made a career on satirical hoaxes and fakes, address one of the most disorienting realizations about the current historical period, increasingly shared by journalists, politicians, academics and

---

[1] Pulver, A. (2019). "Sacha Baron Cohen: Facebook would have let Hitler buy ads for 'final solution'". *The Guardian*. https://www.theguardian.com/film/2019/nov/22/sacha-baron-cohen-facebook-would-have-sold-final-solution-ads-to-hitler.

concerned citizens alike: we now live in a post-truth[2] world, where emotions and beliefs trump evidence-based arguments, where the distinction between truth and lies has become increasingly blurred, and where the very notion of truth seems to have all but disappeared. Such world, primarily operating on social media, is taking more and more dystopian contours.

In the aftermath of the upsetting outcome of Brexit referendum, which has plunged the UK into prolonged political disorder, and the even more shocking result of US 2016 presidential elections, which propelled Donald Trump, a controversial businessman with a dubious financial record and penchant for lying,[3] to the highest political position in the world, scholars and media observers were taken aback by what they saw as an epistemic crisis that had struck at the heart of Western democracies and media systems. Since then, a plurality of analyses and theoretical arguments has been offered to identify and make sense of what has been defined as a 'post-truth condition.' Post-truth as a cultural and political condition can be observed in several phenomena that have recently emerged in Western countries, such as the circulation of intentionally or unintentionally misleading or false information via the Internet by and among an increasingly polarized and emotional public opinion; the political communication and influence strategies based on manipulation and deception by State and non-State actors by means of trolls,[4] political bots[5] and other forms of computational propaganda[6]; and also in the

---

[2] Following the now standard definition of the Oxford Dictionaries, which in 2016 awarded 'post-truth' the title of word of the year, the term can be defined as a social and political condition in which appeals to emotions and beliefs supersede rational or fact-based arguments, thus leading citizens and politicians to no longer respect objective truths. See https://en.oxforddictionaries.com/definition/post-truth.

[3] Kessler, G., et al. (2019). "President Trump has made 10,796 false or misleading claims over 869 days". *The Washington Post.* https://www.washingtonpost.com/politics/2019/06/10/president-trump-has-made-false-or-misleading-claims-over-days/?utm_term=.fa1bf3f96ff5.

[4] "Trolling can refer to relatively innocuous pranks, but it can also take the form of more serious behaviors. (…) In practice, however, trolling has grown to serve as an umbrella term which encompasses a wide variety of asocial internet behaviors" (Marwick and Lewis 2017, 4).

[5] "Political bots are software agents used to generate simple messages and 'conversations' on social media" (Woolley and Howard 2018, 3).

[6] "Computational propaganda describes the use of algorithms, automation and human curation to purposefully manage and distribute misleading information over social media networks" (ibid., 4).

industry of political marketing relying on cognitive-behavioral science, big data analysis and micro-targeting. These examples of post-truth communications occur in a media and political context, increasingly centered on social media, that has evolved to incentivize such forms of strategic manipulations of citizens and of the public opinion.

However, post-truth is not simply a Western phenomenon, but it is also affecting multiple parts of the world. On-line rumors, Internet hoaxes, Facebook fakes, inflammatory memes, conspiracy theories via anonymous imageboard and disinformation campaigns by Twitter shape and affect political discourses and events across the globe, from Myanmar to Russia, from Syria to Brazil. Still, most discussions of post-truth tend to have a Western-centric focus. British journalist D'Ancona (2017) decries the 'declining value of truth' in a political era where emotional narratives are reclaiming primacy in public conversations at the expense of factual and verifiable arguments. In his analysis, D'Ancona locates the source of the problem in the 'fragility' of Western democratic institutions and in a crisis of trust suffered by traditional sources of authority and information, such as political parties and the press, which accelerated after the emergence of new media technologies, particularly social media, and was compounded by the 2008 economic recession. American literary critic Kakutani (2018) is equally wary of the emergence of the post-truth era and laments the 'perfect storm' of political, cultural and technological factors that have created the condition for the rise of a post-truth politician such as Trump. In her discussion, post-truth appears as a broader societal malaise whose causes are to be traced back to the sociopolitical transformations of the 1960s, to the culture wars that ensued afterward, to the postmodern sensibility questioning grand political narratives, which has now spread from the left to the right of the political spectrum, as well as to the rise in the importance of subjectivity in public conversations, to the detriment of objective truth.

Academics have also grappled with the polymorphic nature of the post-truth problem for a while now. The complex phenomenon is often discussed by analyzing a set of interrelated aspects which recur in many of the accounts and theoretical arguments offered by the scholarly community. Social media are often placed at the center of such discussions, with scholars such as Vaidhyanathan (2018) offering a rather critical assessment of the disruption caused particularly by Facebook on public discourse and political communications. The platform's economic model, the logic of its algorithm and the psychological incentives it generates are seen as culprits for the problems of political polarization, the 'siloing' of users into cognitive and cultural echo-chambers and the circulation of various forms of false information. McIntyre (2018) and Salgado (2018) also engage with the role of social media as drivers of post-truth politics, but through analyses which include, among other things, a discussion of postmodern cultural relativism as antecedent to the current post-truth era. Harsin (2018) also discusses the postmodern epistemic fragmentation of truth as a precondition to the current post-truth era, but similarly to D'Ancona, he emphasizes the declining trust in mediating authorities as the ultimate causal factor behind the deterioration of truth in public discourses.

Academic discussions on post-truth also identify its preconditions in the broader historical transformations of the media systems and of journalism since the 1990s, which have led to increased fragmentation of news outlets along ideological orientations in order to compete for demographic segments and audience attention, to the hybridization of information and entertainment and to the rise of opinion journalism at the expense of factual and investigative reporting. The unique brand of partisan and opinionated journalism that emerged over talk radio (Cosentino (2017) and the 'pernicious objectivity' pursued by cable news programs hungry for ratings are considered by D'Ancona (2017) as conducive to the trust crisis currently plaguing legacy news media.

Discussing the issue of political polarization from an American perspective, Benkler et al. (2018) and Bennett and Livingston (2018) identify an asymmetry in such polarization whereby the traditional right-wing media, such as Fox News, and alternative media outlets affiliated with the 'alt-right,'[7] such as Breitbart News, have a much greater responsibility in the spreading of false or inaccurate information than their liberal competitors. Contributing to such asymmetry is also the emerging ecosystem of subcultural practices that fall under the umbrella term of 'trolling' (Marwick and Lewis 2017; Nagle 2017; Hannan 2018), which have spawned out

---

[7] The term alt-right was coined in the US context to identify a loose aggregation of right-wing and far-right political movements standing in opposition to the authority of the Republican establishment and to liberal and progressive politics. The main feature of the alt-right is to operate primarily on-line, relying on a sophisticated knowledge of the technological, political and cultural dynamics of the Internet. While alt-right members distance themselves from traditional neo-Nazism or racism, the movement is considered to be a media savvy rebranding of the traditional White supremacist ideology (Marwick and Lewis 2017).

of imageboard platforms and discussion forums such as 4chan,[8] 8chan
and Reddit and have given shape to a far-right on-line political discourse
through a wild mixture of hoaxes and memes.[9]

The emerging conceptual framework on post-truth politics also
includes discussions on the crisis of democracy and the rise of populism,
as per the already mentioned work by Bennett and Livingston (2018)
and Kakutani (2018), as well as by Waisbord (2018). Populism as both a
political project and political language (Kazin 2016; Judis 2016; Revelli
2019) has proved permeable to a tendency of "elevating appeals to fear
and anger over reasoned debate, eroding democratic institutions, and
replacing expertise with the wisdom of the crowd" (Kakutani 2018, 14).
Established trends of political communication embracing self-branding
and 'promotionalism' (Harsin 2018; Kalpokas 2018), so-called celebrifi-
cation (Corner and Pels 2003) and entertaining politics (Baym and Jones
2012) are also considered at the roots a gradual deterioration in the political discourse.

In the theoretical contribution offered by Kalpokas (2018), 'promotionalism' is not only confined to the political realm, but it is instead
seen as a part of a broader societal tendency toward the self-promotion
and self-branding practices that are incentivized by the operational logics of social media. Kalpokas pushes this idea further conceptualizing
post-truth as being based on narratives or 'escapist fictions,' which are
imbued with affective and aspirational values. Contrary to most academic
accounts, Kalpokas doesn't consider post-truth as an inherently negative
phenomenon. While at times his analysis appears politically ambiguous,
falling short of denouncing falsities and manipulations, he nonetheless
recognizes agency in the publics who participate to post-truth, a position which is best summed up by the following quote: "Post-truth is not
manipulation of some sort—it is collusion" (Kalpokas 2018, 18).

[8] 4chan and 8chan are Internet forums or discussion boards based on the sharing
of images and comments by mostly anonymous users. 4chan and 8chan are credited
for having popularized terms, jokes and memes which have become staples of on-line
subcultures as well as of the broader popular culture. Since the mid-2000s, 4chan has
also been the breeding ground and meeting place for the notorious group of hackers and
activists that gather under the collective pseudonym Anonymous, whose name is derived
from the ability of users to post messages anonymously on the imageboard.

[9] "In modern internet parlance, a meme is a visual trope that proliferates across Internet
spaces as it is replicated and altered by anonymous users" (Marwick and Lewis 2017, 36).

Finally, contributing to the broader definition of post-truth politics, there is also the academic literature on disinformation and computational propaganda, which focuses on the role of political parties and movements, on the activities of agents officially or unofficially affiliated with State actors, as well as on the actions by terrorist organizations, in the production and distribution of false or misleading information for manipulative and propagandistic ends, often with the help of software automation. The most widespread and advanced forms of social media manipulation at the service of influence operations are to be credited to Russian hackers and trolls, especially in the carefully orchestrated strategy aimed at interfering with the 2016 US elections (Benkler et al. 2018; DiResta et al. 2018; Woolley and Howard 2018).

While the theory on post-truth is beginning to find coherent systematization as per the ideas and the works mentioned above, which will be discussed in greater detail in the next sections, there are nonetheless some aspects of the phenomenon that haven't been adequately addressed. What appears to be missing in the current literature on post-truth is a discussion of the problem that adopts a comparative global perspective, and which uses, tests and, if necessary, develops the existing theory through the analyses of different global case studies. This book aims at filling this gap, and to this end, it presents a comparative critical discussion of a series of examples that bear witness of the global diffusion of post-truth politics via social media and the Internet.

This research project aims at investigating patterns of continuity and correlations in global post-truth practices and to flesh out broader geopolitical trends engendered by post-truth politics, by looking at the co-production and circulation of false and manipulative narratives across multiple world regions, while at the same time appreciating the specificity of each case study. In particular, I am interested in unearthing the flows of disinformation enabled by the networked relations among State and non-State actors across multiple platforms, regions and continents, as seen in multiple recent examples such as Kremlin-backed Russian news networks amplifying the contentious views of alt-right American activists, and vice versa, or American and European youths circulating memes in support of Middle-Eastern dictators. An important comparative work on disinformation was recently compiled by researchers of computational propaganda (Woolley and Howard 2018), which, while presenting a rich selection of empirical analyses, doesn't, however, locate the problem of disinformation within the post-truth academic discussion and doesn't provide a theoretical elaboration of its historical, cultural and philosophical preconditions.

The discussion of post-truth informing this book necessarily foregrounds the transformative and disruptive impact of social media such as Facebook, Twitter and YouTube—and the Internet more generally—on political communications and public discourse in various world regions. The analysis, however, steers clear of technological deterministic arguments. Rather, the book discusses social media as a communication technology steeped into political-economic contexts and embedded with distinct ideological and cultural features. If "the epistemic nature of facts has become frailer and more contested" (Salgado 2018, 321), and if mediating authorities are less able as act as truth-arbiters (Harsin 2018), social media are enhancing already existing cultural and political dynamics at the roots of the post-truth condition. The spread of fictional political narratives, the rampant anti-elitist and anti-expert rhetoric,[10] the rise of right-wing populist leaders and political movements in Europe, the United States and elsewhere, as well as the strengthening of authoritarian regimes and the related decline of the liberal democratic model, are discussed in the book as parts of the broader historical context to which post-truth politics are contributing.

Following the theoretical elaborations previously mentioned, the conceptual starting point upon which I base my analysis is that the current epistemic crisis that is affecting multiple political contexts—leading to increasing inability for people around the world to tell the truth from fiction, and for public opinions to reach a deliberative consensus grounded on a shared view of reality—is not only linked to technological and cultural transformations brought by social media platforms, but is the offshoot of a broader crisis of trust and authority of mainstream Western media and political institutions in the global geopolitical arena.[11]

As argued by D'Ancona a "collapse of trust is the social basis of the Post-Truth era" (D'Ancona 2017, 36). Liberal democracy and its

---

[10] During the campaign preceding the Brexit referendum, British MP Michael Gove famously argued that "people in this country have had enough of experts". See Mance, H. (2016). "Britain has had enough of experts, says Gove". *Financial Times.* https://www.ft.com/content/3be49734-29cb-11e6-83e4-abc22d5d108c.

[11] Following the definition offered by Tuathail et al. (2006), geopolitics can be defined as "a discourse about world politics, with a particular emphasis on state competition and the geographical dimensions of power".

main institutions are suffering a 'fiduciary' (Harsin 2018) or trust crisis, and consequently, such formerly established global truth-arbiters face the mounting epistemic and ideological challenges posed by previously secondary or marginalized political actors, both at the domestic level and at the international level. This problem is in fact not limited to the Western world, but as Benkler et al. argue, the crisis of liberal democracy is concerning many countries "from the Philippines, through India, to Turkey" which "saw shifts from liberal democratic forms to a new model of illiberal, and in some cases authoritarian, majoritarianism" (Benkler et al. 2018, 4).

The main contribution of this book is thus the application of existing conceptualization of post-truth on a broader global scale. To this end, this book aims at analyzing and discussing post-truth as a social and political condition with geopolitical implications, which manifests itself across different countries and plays an important role in the power relations and struggles among different State actors, and ultimately impacts the very course of the broader globalization process. The book attempts at broadening the geopolitical understanding of the phenomenon by looking at how post-truth serves as a space of ideological confrontation between elite and non-elite societal formations, as well as an opportunity for State actors of covertly exerting influence on rival countries in the context of elections or armed conflicts.

In other words, I am framing post-truth as qualitatively different from earlier ways of influence-making for resource-rich State and grassroots non-State actors, occurring in a global context where established power relations are currently being subject to significant redefinition, particularly in the aftermath of the Trump and Brexit upsets. As an example, Russia is clearly exploiting the post-truth condition, by means of influence and disinformation campaigns, to advance its geopolitical agenda in multiple world regions, from Europe to the United States, as well as in the Middle East and Africa, as part of a broader strategy to undermine the democratic process of rival countries, as well as to advance its own vision for a renewed imperialism and military expansionism.

Russian tactics and strategies occur in lockstep with a concomitant crisis in the global appeal of Western liberal democracy. In my reading, the breakdown in social trust previously enjoyed by established institutions of twentieth-century liberal democracies—mass parties, the media, educational and scientific institutions—is happening against the backdrop of a broader trust crisis in Western global hegemony and Western-led glob-alization, as well as in the neoliberal[12] consensus on democracy and free-market capitalism that has dominated global politics over the course of the past quarter century. This is the historical and geopolitical perimeter that needs to be established in order to understand the post-truth crisis suffered by Western media and political institutions, in both the national and international arenas. As a periodizing concept, post-truth is thus use-ful insofar it describes a historical phase that signals the crisis of Western democratic institutions to act as truth-arbiters in matters of domestic pub-lic affairs, as well as the demise of Western and more specifically Anglo-American hegemony over world politics and culture.

The collapse of the Soviet Union and the following emergence in the 1990s and early 2000s of the United States as the single remain-ing superpower established the Western 'modernity package' of liberal democracy and free-market capitalism driven by consumerism as a global ideological model, and the last grand narrative of the twentieth century, promoted by the 'regime of truth'[13] (Foucault 1976/2000) circulated by Western television networks and culture industries. Such hegemonic epistemic perspective on society, economics and politics overshadowed those of competing ideological traditions—for example Marxist or Euro-pean social democratic—and it was presented to former Soviet countries and to countries in the Global South as the ready-made recipe for eco-nomic growth and political stability. Over the course of the past three decades, the neoliberal turn taken by Western democracies, coupled with the growing global networked interconnectedness and the globalization of economies and cultures, pushed even further the reach and authority of the Western globalization discourse as a totalizing ideology (Mattelart 2002).

However, the twenty-first century brought an unexpected reality check to Fukuyama's 'end of history' narrative that permeated the 'globaliza-tion as westernization' paradigm in the 1990s (Fukuyama 1992; Pieterse

[12] For a definition of neoliberalism see Harvey (2005): "Neoliberalism is in the first instance a theory of political economic practices that proposes that human well-being can best be advanced by liberating individual entrepreneurial freedoms and skills within an institutional framework characterized by strong private property rights, free markets and free trade" (Harvey 2005, 2).

[13] By 'regimes of truth' Foucault meant the types of discourse which a society 'accepts and makes function as true,' as well as the issues and locus of political debate and social confrontation.

2003). The correlation between the expansion of liberal democracy and free-market capitalism alongside the development of a global media system was challenged by the growing complexity and instability of such globalized and networked communication system. McNair (2008) spoke of the ensuing cultural chaos inherent in the emerging global media environment, which he saw as characterized by the loss of control by political and cultural elites. Expanded and accelerated information flows brought by 24/7 news channels, and the rise of interactivity and mass participation in the form of citizen journalism and user-generated content made possible by the Internet created a 'globalized public sphere' which turned out much more difficult to manage and police by established powers. Scandals, public relations crisis, leaks, unauthorized releases of confidential or classified information and whistleblowing have become the staples of the unfiltered, constant flow of information disseminated by hypercompetitive corporate media and amateur or activist news outlets alike. McNair's position could now be criticized for being too optimistic and naive, part of a widespread belief in the grassroots democratization enabled by the Internet that was still popular in the early 2000s. Such views are difficult to sustain nowadays, especially in light of more recent events such as the Cambridge Analytica scandal,[14] which demonstrated how financial and political elites could coordinate to acquire, control and exploit people's digital profiles and activities on the Internet.

Nonetheless, it can't be denied that Habermas model of public sphere (Habermas 1991), one of the pillars of modernity and democracy, is undergoing further transformation with recent social changes and technological advancements, and it is being both extended on a more global scale and fractured into a plurality of discursive subsets, or bubbles, that slide away from a centralized and elite-steered consensus to engender diasporic and alternative spaces for political aggregation and mobilization. Such global and fragmented public sphere also lends itself to the manipulation and cannibalization by rogue actors, both domestic and international. State and non-State actors, as well as groups of citizens, jointly collaborate to the production of post-truth narratives with the goal of subverting established political, scientific and cultural orders and of exploiting the

[14] Cadwalldr, C. (2017). "Follow the data: Does a legal document link Brexit campaigns to US billionaire?". *The Guardian*. https://www.theguardian.com/technology/2017/may/14/robert-mercer-cambridge-analytica-leave-eu-referendum-brexit-campaigns.

peculiar and volatile technological, political and cultural conditions of the current era to wage information wars and ideological battles.

The collective trauma of 9/11, the setbacks suffered by the neoliberal consensus in the aftermath of the 2008 financial crisis—which sent multiple Western countries into recession—the debacle of the 2003 Iraq War and the consequent rise of Islamic fundamentalism in the Middle East and elsewhere, as well as the more recent authoritarian backlash against the Arab Spring, most notably in Egypt, Libya and Syria, have challenged at the core the supremacy of the American-led Western ideological project. A "trust decline after the 2008 recession (but also the Iraq war)" led to hostility to the globalized economy "shifting from the fringes to the center of political discourse. It became commonplace to question an economic system initially presented as a reliable source of rising prosperity that now seemed horribly vulnerable to the caprice of its operating elite" (D'Ancona 2017, 37).

Disenfranchised demographics began to resist the 'regime of truth' enforced by centrist, technocratic politicians and to reject the rhetoric of globalization and neoliberal democracy, which are deemed as culprits of rising inequalities. Right-wing nationalist parties in Europe tapped into this discontent, making significant electoral gains. Both at the domestic and at the global level, the stability of the neoliberal democratic media and political establishments has been fundamentally challenged by competing and dissenting voices—from the so-called alt-right in the United States to nationalist populism in Europe—which have been amplified and made more relevant by independent on-line media ecosystems.

The globalist liberal 'ideoscape,' or ideological space (Appadurai 1990), is on a collision course against a plurality of smaller, yet interconnected, ethnonationalist and conservative ideoscapes empowered by social media. Appadurai, in the earlier phase of the academic debate on cultural globalization, already spoke of the globalized world as 'rhizomic and schizophrenic,' characterized by a disjuncture between 'fantasies' of vicinity and homogenization on the one hand and 'alienation and psychological distance' on the other (Appadurai 1990, 323). Such disjuncture could be seen as a conceptual precursor of the emerging post-truth global age, and it could thus be argued that from a geopolitical perspective, the advent of the post-truth era signals the crisis of the neoliberal and American-led Western globalization project.

Post-truth is also linked to changes in the very dynamics between ideological apparatuses and political discourses, both at the national and at the global level, and to the communication technologies that enable such dynamics. Networked digital media, particularly social media platforms, have become the fastest growing vehicle for political communication worldwide—for campaigning, information-sharing and citizens' mobilization—and their transformative impact is currently being assessed in both its positive and negative implications. From the innovative campaign of Obama in 2008 to the historical wave of demonstrations of the Arab Spring in 2011 until the controversial election of Donald Trump in 2016, scholars, politicians and journalists have become aware of the paradigm-shifting effects that the social networking platforms are wielding on politics and societies.

The general optimistic expectations on the role of network technologies and digital media in enabling new forms of organization, collaboration and political action spread as an integral part of the broader globalization rhetoric, as the features embedded in Web 2.0 platforms appeared to be conducive to both democratic empowerment and new entrepreneurial opportunities. However, lack of knowledge of the long-term and structural impact of the Internet on society and politics, and a certain degree of naïve enthusiasm, led many to embrace uncritically or too optimistically the advent of the new media era as the dawning of a period of liberating direct democracy and of a McLuhanesque 'global village.' During the past years, it has become evident that the very set of incentives that have turned social media into successful and pervasive global missionaries of digital communicative capitalism (Dean 2010) has also had troubling consequences in the way they affect citizens' discussions of public affairs, their interaction with politicians, their process of political identity formation and their access to information on domestic or global affairs.

Furthermore, the adoption of social media platforms in different local contexts has generated unexpected outcomes. The tools and resources that only a few years ago were hailed for furthering democratization and liberating countries from dictators, like in the Middle East and North Africa, have promptly been turned into weapons at the service of terrorists and autocrats (Tufecki 2017). Western democracies have also proven to be vulnerable. The platforms invented in the United States to facilitate connection and communication have been weaponized and turned into channels of malicious content against the democratic institutions of the very country which created them, as seen in the Russian information warfare and influence campaigns during the 2016 US elections (DiResta et al. 2018; Woolley and Howard 2018).

It took the earth-shaking shocks of the Trump election and of Brexit, whose ripple effects still reverberate to this day, for the broader public opinion, the media establishment and academic community in the United States and Europe to realize that social media—in alignment with other factors—could have a major role in upending, almost overnight, political arrangements and power structures of the twentieth century.[15] Both the Trump victory and Brexit are often presented as examples of post-truth politics because of the role played in their unfolding by disinformation and misinformation, spread by multiple agents across a plurality of channels, with ramifications across the globe. Drawing concepts from Harsin (2015), it could be argued that after Brexit and Trump, the Western world is moving from a relatively stable 'regime of truth,' dating back to the 1980s and upheld by the neoliberal democratic order, to a still unknown and unpredictable 'regime of post-truth,' characterized by resurrecting global powers such as Russia, the rising geopolitical profile of China and the emergence of a plurality of nationalistic autocratic leaders. The initial reaction to these political events was to point the finger against the Internet and social media, which were blamed for facilitating the spreading of disinformation among disaffected citizens, for enabling ideological echo-chambers and for leading to a polarization of the public opinion. Innovations in the media system and political communication were, however, but one dimension of the structural changes that occurred in Western liberal democracies over the past decade. Broader financial, cultural and geopolitical factors were also involved: the economic changes brought forth by globalization, the destabilizing effects of neoliberal policies on many sectors and recent financial turmoil drove important wedges among privileged and underprivileged sections of many societies, both in the United States and in Europe, as well of course between affluent and developing countries. Migration flows from war-torn or poverty-stricken regions of the Global South have caused anxieties in the countries of destination, concerned about the security and identity issues that uncontrolled immigration flows could engender (Inglehart and Norris 2016). Furthermore, the political and military institutions that served as guarantors of

---

[15] Jaishankar, D. (2016). "Brexit: The first major casualty of digital democracy". *Brookings Institute.* https://www.brookings.edu/blog/order-from-chaos/2016/06/29/brexit-the-first-major-casualty-of-digital-democracy/.

stability and order in the Atlantic area and in Europe, such NATO and the EU, are facing a mounting challenge by hostile State actors like Russia, particularly under Putin's third term as president (Pomerantsev and Weiss 2014; Van Herpen 2016). Hailing the role of all-news Russian network *RT*—formerly *Russia Today*—in presenting alternative perspectives on world affairs, Putin himself spoke of Russia's goal to "break the Anglo-Saxon monopoly on global information streams" and to challenge the ideological hegemony of global Western media outlets such as the *BBC* and *CNN*.[16]

Therefore, the issue of post-truth can't simply be treated from a media-centric perspective, but it should instead be analyzed through a theoretical prism built on economic, social, cultural and geopolitical considerations. The book will then start, particularly in the coming section, by discussing the concept of post-truth as a phenomenon first observed and conceptualized by journalists and scholars within the Western context, analyzing its different facets and linking its genealogy to structural transformations in political communication and in the media/politics nexus during the past decades. Such theoretical discussion of post-truth will then be applied in the following chapters to examples from various world regions.

Over the course of a decade, social media platforms have become dominant global media actors, allowing for cultural and political practices and discourses to be produced and shared irrespectively of national borders. Right-wing populist politics, for example, have thrived in the social media and alternative information ecosystems, spreading quickly across the Atlantic and feeding its different local instantiations with a common set of symbols, themes and narratives on issues such as the opposition to immigration, border protection and the defense of Judeo-Christian values. A popular narrative frame in this ideological milieu—the 'false flag'[17] trope common to many conspiracy theories—can equally be spotted in

[16] Rutenberg, J. (2017). "RT, Sputnik and Russia's New Theory of War". *The New York Times Magazine*. https://www.nytimes.com/2017/09/13/magazine/rt-sputnik-and-russias-new-theory-of-war.html.

[17] False flag narratives suggest the existence of covert operations, often by government agencies, behind events such as mass shootings or terrorist actions, which are alleged to be either staged or purposely conducted in order to exploit the ensuing public outrage to implement political agendas. An example would be unsubstantiated allegations, popularized by conspiracists such as Alex Jones, that the 2012 Sandy Hook mass shooting was staged in order to enforce stricter gun control regulation. See Williamson, E. (2018). "Truth in a post-truth era: Sandy Hook families Sue Alex Jones, conspiracy theorist".

the discourse of right-wing activists opposing gun control in the United States as well as in the on-line conversations of Russian and international media supporting the Syrian regime. The flows of post-truth cultural and political practices enabled by global social media are thus creating a plurality of epistemic ruptures and crises in multiple local contexts, which are exacerbated and exploited by influence operations by State actors, such as the covert media manipulation campaigns carried by the Kremlin-backed Internet Research Agency (IRA).[18] The global post-truth condition is also reinforced by the spontaneous circulation of fictional political narratives, such as the conspiracy theories concocted and spread by social media users.

The goal of the book is thus to unearth the power relations and the cultural and ideological tensions operating at multiple levels—from the grassroots level to the broader international context—that intersect the issue of post-truth, which is discussed as a cultural and political condition with an increasingly global reach. To this end, the book will attempt to provide a coherent and unifying reading of the issue by drawing on a plurality of theoretical contributions which will be applied to a series of case studies chosen for their political relevance, and because they jointly paint a picture of crisis in the global hegemony of Western liberal democracy. Through this far-reaching discussion, the book will attempt to sketch a map, necessarily rough and incomplete, but detailed enough to help readers navigate the uncharted grounds of the post-truth world order.

1.2   The Post-truth Condition

Deception and manipulation in the form of lies and propaganda are as old as politics and have been object of academic inquiry for decades. Hannah Arendt famously wrote that "no one (…) has ever counted truthfulness among the political virtues. Lies have always been regarded as necessary and justifiable tools not only of the politician's or the demagogue's but also of the statesman's trade" (Arendt 1972, 4). Deceptions in politics are thus by no means novelties, as they existed also in the era of mass media

The New York Times. https://www.nytimes.com/2019/12/12/us/politics/sandy-hook-infowars-alex-jones.html.

[18] Isaac, M., & Wakabayashi, D. (2017). "Russian influence reached 126 million through Facebook alone". *The New York Times*. https://www.nytimes.com/2017/10/30/technology/facebook-google-russia.html.

in the form of strategic communications such as war propaganda or even advertising and public relations. What distinguishes the current post-truth era is, however, the reach and the speed that characterize the circulation of deceptive communications. With respect to this, Italian scholar and activist Franco 'Bifo' Berardi argued: "The fake is not a novelty in the public discourse. What is new is the speed, the intensity and the enormous amount of information (true or false) to which the social mind is exposed. The acceleration of the infosphere (…) has saturated the attention and has consequently disabled society's critical abilities."[19]

The notion of post-truth thus updates and introduces new complexity to an age-old problem, and as such, it has become one of the defining concepts of the social media age. In the current post-truth predicament, a key preliminary distinction needs to be drawn between misinformation and disinformation. Misinformation "is the spreading of inaccurate or false information while *mistakenly* thinking one is sharing accurate information", while disinformation is based on "*deliberately* spreading false or inaccurate information" (Harsin 2018, 7). The distinction between the two forms of deception is, however, blurred, as a disinformation campaign might willingly produce misinformed people who in turn unwillingly amplify deliberately false information. Bennett and Livingston also consider disinformation as a useful catch-all concept in discussing post-truth—which they refer to as 'disinformation order'—insofar as the term "invites looking at more systematic disruptions of authoritative information flows due to strategic deceptions that may appear very credible to those consuming them" (Bennett and Livingston 2018, 124). Equating disinformation only with strategic deceptions by powerful actors doesn't, however, render the complex, synergic and stratified nature of most post-truth communications, which rely on the active participation of citizens and grassroots initiatives and operate against a backdrop of declining authority of information centers.

In the current literature engaging theoretically and critically with post-truth, a key work that stands out for its thoroughness is the *Post-truth and Critical Communication* entry published by Harsin (2018) in the Oxford Research Encyclopedia of Communication, which presents an examination of the issue from a plurality of perspectives. According to Harsin (2018), at the roots of the post-truth condition, there are two main

---

[19]Berardi, F. (2017). "Verità e simulazione". *Alfabeta2*. https://www.alfabeta2.it/2017/04/09/verita-e-simulazione/ (Translation by the author).

orders of problems: *epistemic* and '*fiduciary.*' Epistemic problems related to competing truth-claims were already inherent in the postmodern critique of twentieth-century grand metanarratives, increasingly unable to steadily anchor meanings to political 'master signifiers' and thus replaced, according to Lyotard by contingent and non-totalizing understandings of social and political reality (Lyotard 1984). The gradual decline of Marxist ideologies and the skepticism toward the claims of the Western Enlightenment project in the post-colonial era are examples of metanarratives in crisis. The postmodern and tactical identity politics that have flourished starting from the late 1970s and early 1980s can be seen as responses to the crisis of metanarratives that began with postmodernism.

The postmodern turn in philosophy was based on a critique of knowledge, beliefs and truths as being coterminous with power structures, and as such instantiated and reproduced through language and discourses. Knowledge and truth, as philosophical and political concepts, were seen as relative to the power dynamics that enabled and constructed them, and as such could be deconstructed and challenged as part of political and ideological conflicts. As summed up by Salgado, who references Lyotard, postmodernism posits that "knowledge and reality are relative to discourse and interplay, which often give rise to contradictory interpretations of reality" (Salgado 2018, 321). Postmodernism is thus a precursor to the ideological fragmentation and cultural relativism of the current era, in which the subjective personal experience of reality supersedes any ontology of a preexisting objective reality.

In his already mentioned discussion of 'regimes of truth,' Foucault linked power and knowledge to argue that knowledge and truth are inherently relative to power structures. Truth for Foucault is the "result of discourse, power relations and context" deriving from "competing systems of discourse, and what is true is determined by which system is dominant and not by which system is correct" (Salgado 2018, 322). In Foucault's interpretation, truth is a construction of power, and since power is historically determined and contingent, there cannot be an absolute truth. Postmodernism thus offers a 'post-factual relativism' which stands as a reaction to the dogmas of modernity, which were built on the political and cultural dominance of rational thought, bureaucratization and science, and on the public trust that the scientific method could deliver widely accepted truths.

The epistemic crisis ushered in by postmodernist relativism could thus be considered as inherently related to the trust or 'fiduciary' crisis (Harsin

2018) suffered by gatekeepers and truth-arbiters of twentieth-century modernity. Harsin doesn't consider postmodern epistemic relativism as foundational of post-truth, but he rather sees the trust crisis suffered by mediating authorities such as journalists as the primary driver of post-truth. This is what, in his reading, differentiates the current post-truth from the precedent postmodern condition of 'truth fragmentation' (Harsin 2015, 2018). The real concern of the present era is that a crisis of the trusted authorities of the past has fostered a social and political condition plagued by suspicions and skepticism, and replete with conflicting narratives, dishonesties, inaccuracies, and false or fabricated information. As the political and economic conditions underpinning previous regimes of truth are challenged by structural transformations in the media/politics nexus, established truth-enforcing institutions lose the support of citizens and audiences, both at the national level and at the broader global level.

The existence of shared truths doesn't simply depend on the verifiability of information and of the evidence that supports it, but also on the trust status of the authority in charge of verifying and arbitering such evidence. If such 'fiduciary' status is challenged, then the distinction between truth and falsity is questioned and compromised too. In my reading, postmodern epistemic relativism and the trust crisis of mediating authorities are inherently related, and the deterioration of objective truth in public discourses is linked to both factors. This is the most radical consequence of the relativizing effect of postmodernity and of its tendency toward fragmenting reality, deconstructing authorities and upsetting dominant narratives: "The fragmentations of the truth, in the subject as well as in the world, if a fundamental axis to comprehend the basis of postmodernity (…) It is not a coincidence that the networked society is permeated by mythologies, dreams and excitements that disarticulate any rational argument and all established or universal morals" (Susca and De Kerckhove 2008, 16).[20] The mythologies of the networked society are the fictional political narratives, the Internet folk tales, the hoaxes, the conspiracy theories and the other forms of post-truth storytelling circulating on-line that pierce through the cracks of established, evidence-based consensual truths, and from there pollinate alternative information ecosystems, overcoming their previous relegation to marginal knowledge and usurping the center of public discourses.

[20] Translation by the author.

Following the Lacanian analysis proposed by Zizek, it could be suggested that legacy media are experiencing a crisis of their 'symbolic' efficiency, that is of their ability to mediate and structure reality, while social media and the Internet more generally are releasing the assault of the 'imaginary' dimension of self-expression of citizens and audiences (Zizek in Dean 2010). This point echoes the argument suggested by Kalpokas in his reading of post-truth as having an emancipatory quality, which endows users and citizens with the ability to create fictional accounts of reality that serve their aspirational needs in the emerging 'Experience Age' engendered by social media (Kalpokas 2018).

The result is an epistemic confusion in which competing systems of knowledge and beliefs, operating nationally and globally, vie for the emotional and cognitive engagement of citizens across multiple networked platforms. This is what Harsin calls a 'regime of post-truth' based on a plurality of competing 'truth-markets': while the Foucauldian 'regime of truth' was produced and transmitted under the control of a small set of dominant media offering a narrow set of authoritative discourses, in the 'regime of post-truth' resource-rich political and economic actors like politicians, media groups, State actors, as well as resources-poor activists and subcultural groups, are engaged in the co-production of competing narratives, with cacophonic and disorienting results.

Such trust crisis is linked also to changes in the dynamics of power and authority in contemporary late-capitalist societies. Unlike older Marxist critiques of culture industries and mass entertainment, à la Frankfurt School, in the post-truth condition, citizens and audiences are not seen as necessarily submissive and passive, a point made by both Harsin (2018) and Kalpokas (2018). On the contrary, the current conception of post-truth emphasizes the contrasts and tensions among elite and non-elite group, a cultural and political opposition which can also be found expressed in the standard rhetoric of contemporary populism (Waisbord 2018; Revelli 2019). Discord on key social and political issues is a site of post-truth tensions, such as the ideological battles around climate change or mandatory vaccination for children, which can be seen as forms of popular insubordination against scientific authorities. At the heart of the trust crisis and of the 'cultural chaos' of post-truth, there is a general inability by traditional elites, challenged by new cultural and political entities, to efficiently manage the different truth-markets available to the publics.

There is of course a complex matrix of factors causing the crisis of these formerly dominant and detached political and media elites, which

are experiencing an encroachment by new political identities and formations. The audiences of the current new media era are made of 'pro-
sumers,' producers/consumers who engage with information in interac-
tive contexts of Web 2.0 platforms, which enable user-generated content
and constant connection, and where access to news happens in economies
of attention heavily charged with emotions. Kalpokas (2018) argues that
such environments foster the "creation of affiliative truth (…) capable
of mobilising audiences" (Kalpokas 2018, 9). Self-expression, cognitive
and emotional engagement and identity formation via social media occur
within specific technological conditions, such as the constraints of algorithmic curation of information flows—for example the Facebook news
feed—and the incentivization of virality via likes and shares, to the detriment of veracity.

Harsin also argues that inherent in regimes of post-truth is the pro-
liferation of 'truth-games,' examples of which are the provocative claims
based on rumors, hoaxes and fakes such as those circulated by proponents
of the Pizzagate or of the QAnon conspiracy theories, which will be discussed in Chapter 3: these actors of truth-games spread their outlandish
claims to appeal to beliefs within specific ideological filter bubbles (Pariser
2011) as well as to engage with the hypercompetitive attention economy
of social media. Truth-claims and truth-games circulate across multiple
networks where users seek gratification, status and identity. The management of such post-truth markets demands constant popular participation
in discursive games, which has led to a sort of 'gamification' of on-line
political experience.

The agents of the new truth-markets—populist leaders, demagogues,
propagandists, activists—are attempting to manage the breakdown of
mass audiences into filter bubbles and to exploit the widespread skepticism toward cultural authorities (Nichols 2017). In Harsin's discussion,
a regime of post-truth is designed to "manage citizen-consumers by having them (a) accept that there is no way ultimately to verify truth, (b)
believe their own truth arbiters in their markets, and subsequently (c)
engage in vigorous counterclaiming and debunking." However, Harsin
concludes that the attempts to debunk and verify are usually fruitless,
since there is no main agreed-upon and trusted public venue in which
an "authority can definitively debunk truths by suturing multiple audi-
ence/market/network segments" (Harsin 2015, 6). The fragmentation
of citizens and audiences, eagerly sought and fought for by competing

truth-tellers, leads to increased political polarization. The lack of common authorities and discourses able to reconcile divisions compounds the problems of partisanship and polarization, which are seen as both causes and consequences of the post-truth condition.

Both postmodernism and the crisis of authority of mediating institutions have thus contributed to a shift in contemporary Western societies toward the effacement of boundaries between expert and non-expert knowledge, between facts and fictions, as well as to the diffusion of relativistic skepticism and 'denialism'[21] in political conversations. Ethics and morals have also become relative to one's subjective experience, since the emphasis of political conversations is not on agreed-upon narratives, visions and value-systems, but rather on pragmatic approaches to reality that result in fragmentation, diversity and on the partiality of discourses on truth and reality (Salgado 2018). Going down such a slippery epistemic slope, facts also become social constructions, and not measurable results of objective experience. This ultra-relativistic, liquid approach to political reality is what led Trump lawyer Rudy Giuliani to infamously say that "truth isn't truth."[22]

1.3   FORMS AND FUNCTIONS OF POST-TRUTH

Harsin identifies three main forms of deceptive communication—rumor bombs, fake news and lies—as examples of the current post-truth phenomenon. Harsin (2018) compares rumor bombs to "statements whose veracity is unknown or unprovable, and to communication bombs as longtime forms of information warfare migrating from military to politics" (Harsin 2018, 8). Rumors bombs can be elaborate, contradictory and contain ambiguous claims, so that to generate confusion and disagreement among the public opinion. Rumor bombs can break into the news-cycle after emerging from the subcultural fringes of the Internet or can be spread by professionalized disinformation campaigns in the context of political campaigns or military conflicts.

---

[21] Khan-Harris, K. (2018). "Denialism: What drives people to reject the truth". *The Guardian*. https://www.theguardian.com/news/2018/aug/03/denialism-what-drives-people-to-reject-the-truth.

[22] Pilkington, E. (2018). "'Truth isn't truth': Giuliani trumps 'alternative facts' with new Orwellian outburst". *The Guardian*. https://www.theguardian.com/us-news/2018/aug/19/truth-isnt-truth-rudy-giuliani-trump-alternative-facts-orwellian.

An example of a rumor bomb that worked as a preamble to the current post-truth era—and perhaps not incidentally jumpstarted the political career of Donald Trump[23]—is the 2011 'birther' conspiracy theory against Obama, based on the rumor that he was not born in the United States and thus didn't meet the requirement to be president. While in the 2008 election cycle the rumor remained confined to the periphery of the political conversation, after 2011 the birthers campaign started to be amplified by prominent bloggers and social media, which elevated its visibility, until it was brought into the mainstream by Donald Trump.[24] As it is often the case in post-truth politics, the debunking of the rumor didn't completely displace it from the public conversation.[25] Another example or a rumor bomb is the Pizzagate conspiracy theory targeting Hillary Clinton in the period before the 2016 election. Unlike fake news, which is entirely false, rumors can turn out to be true or contain a modicum of truth. The Pizzagate conspiracy theory, based on rumors alleging that Hillary Clinton was part of a pedophiles' ring active in Washington DC, contained references to the case of convicted pedophile and sex offender Jeffrey Epstein, who had had established relations with Bill Clinton.

Fake news is the most popular sub-category of the broader post-truth phenomenon. Unlike rumor bombs, fake news is patently false or fabricated statements. The term became popular between 2015 and 2016,

---

[23] Gopnik, A. (2015). "Trump and Obama: A night to remember". *The New Yorker.* http://www.newyorker.com/news/daily-comment/trump-and-obama-a-night-to-remember.

[24] The conspiracy theory, which started to spread as early as 2007, before the popularity of social media, relied on speculations circulating via chain emails and blogs. It allegedly started among Hillary Clinton supporters and later spread among followers of the Tea Party movement, eventually reaching the mainstream Republican constituency. The popularity of the Birthers movement is telling of how easily, in the current cultural and technological scenario, rumors can be 'weaponized' in order to mount a political attack. While in the past the gate-keeping function of mainstream media might have effectively prevented the birth certificate rumor to enter the public conversation, Obama felt compelled to address it by publicly displaying his birth certificate, thus amplifying the rumor and making it a legitimate topic of media coverage. For a more thorough discussion of this, see Cosentino (2017).

[25] Even after Obama's display of the birth certificate, a Gallup poll in 2011 showed that one quarter of Republicans were still uncertain about Obama's citizenship. See Morales, L. (2011). "Obama's birth certificate convinces some, but not all, skeptics". *Gallup.* https://news.gallup.com/poll/147530/obama-birth-certificate-convinces-not-skeptics.aspx.

during the Brexit campaign and the 2016 US elections, as a catch-all category identifying various forms of disinformation and misinformation. The term later lost part of its original meaning as various politicians, including Trump, started to use it to dismiss unfavorable coverage and criticism by the media or political opponents. Some academics have cautioned against using the term in relation to post-truth because it frames the problem as isolated incidents of falsehood (Bennett and Livingston 2018), while others have criticized its opaqueness and the political connotations that it has acquired (Benkler et al. 2018). Fake news has also been used to identify producers of false information whose only intention is to leverage on the social media economy of attention simply in order to generate profit, like in the well-known case of the Macedonian fake news factories.[26] Such type of fake or junk news, despite their lack of political intentions, can nonetheless engender political effects, by entering amplification channels of politically motivated actors.

It is worth pointing out that the term fake news was originally associated with satire news program blending information and entertainment such as *The Daily Show* with John Stewart and *The Colbert Report* (Baym and Jones 2012). John Stewart famously attacked CNN in 2004, blaming legacy media for their failure to perform a necessary watchdog function on the US government decisions in a sensitive moment such as the post-9/11 period. The critique of mainstream news brought forth by satire news shows can thus be seen as a precursor of the current trust crisis of journalism and of the traditional media outlets. For two decades, satire news programs have revealed the shortcomings and the codependency of traditional media vis-à-vis the political establishment, instilling in people's mind the suspicion that news was packaged as products to be sold, and that journalistic objectivity was a fabricated myth. *Striscia la Notizia*, a pioneer in satire news in Italy, was launched exactly with the goal of challenging the authority of official news programs on the State broadcaster Rai and to legitimize Berlusconi's commercial television networks. The show's main producer, Antonio Ricci, was one of the first writers for stand-up comedian and later populist politician Beppe Grillo, co-founder of the Five Star Movement party, which has risen to power tapping on people's distrust toward political and cultural elites.

[26] Subramanian, S. (2017). "The Macedonian teens who mastered fake news". *Wired*. https://www.wired.com/2017/02/veles-macedonia-fake-news.

The 'postmodern' and skeptical spectator of satire news shows is thus aware, at times cynically, that mediated reality is a construct. An important aspect of the postmodern sensibility lies in its fascination with the process of representation, which is often exposed and deconstructed to reveal the 'behind the scene,' the marks of authorship and the blurring of the border between stage and backstage. The audience becomes knowledgeable and skeptical of televisual representations, suspicious even, and thus transfers trust onto new and alternative means of mediation and information that acknowledge this postmodern sensibility. Legacy news media is thus challenged by satire news programs or by on-line independent news outlets, while the political outsider is preferred to the professional politician. Populist leader like former Italian Prime Minister Silvio Berlusconi—himself a television tycoon, thus well versed in the logic of spectacle and entertainment—was one of the first to intercept this cultural disposition and tap on it to build a new brand of postmodern politics (Cosentino and Doyle 2010). In a similar vein, Trump, a former reality TV host and a savvy user of media, has titillated popular discontent posing as a political outsider claiming to take on the corruption and inefficiencies of the political establishment.

As for the third sub-category, lying, Harsin sees it as inherently associated with the post-truth condition, whose most visible feature is the noticeable increase of deceptive communications and of discourses around lies and deception, as well as of the instruments and services like fact-checking or rumor-debunking web sites, which are part of the new economy of 'truth-markets' (Harsin 2018). Lies and deceptions can also be seen as structurally inherent in contemporary political communication and journalistic practices, as the logic of entertainment has influenced politics and journalism to the point that tactics of performance, seduction and visibility are emphasized and cultivated to the detriment of truthfulness and honesty.

As mentioned, post-truth has also been also frequently associated with the emergence of populism in the United States and Europe (Waisbord 2018). Populism as a political and rhetorical strategy functions according to a twofold strategy: pitting an idealized and unified 'people' against an equally abstract notion of the elite, and then claiming to be the unfiltered and unbiased representative of the people's will (Kazin 2016).

In his discussion of the relation between populism and post-truth politics, Waisbord argues that the former stands in direct opposition to democratic communications as it "negates the possibility of truth-seeking as a collective goal" (Waisbord 2018, 28). While Waisbord conceptualization of democratic communications appears too normative to be applied realistically to contemporary politics, he rightfully points that that 'populist truth' is always unapologetically partial, partisan and ideological, predicated on the affirmation of 'popular truth.' The *regime of truth* of liberal democracy is thus discarded in favor of a supposedly unfiltered and unmediated 'vox populi,' seen as a truth emerging spontaneously from the people to challenge entrenched powers. In the current tension between populist and liberal democratic politics, the notion of fake news becomes a 'floating signifier' (Farkas and Schou 2018) used flexibly to attack opponents and to establish hegemony over politics and political discourses.

The historical process that led to the current subversion by populist forces of the equilibria in liberal or social democracies has of course deep structural roots, which overlap with those identified as conducive to the post-truth condition. As seen before, the technological, cultural and social transformations occurred at the turn of the millennium have eroded the stability of the institutions and categories of modernity. Such erosive effects have accelerated since the early 1980s in lockstep with the dynamics inherent in late capitalism and postmodernity previously discussed. The categories of modernity have undergone redefinition and have found themselves reshuffled into a disruptive and creative recombination. The result is an explosion into the mainstream of ideas, approaches, visions and values that in the recent past had been confined to the fringes of the public discourse, relegated to the private sphere, even in secret or forbidden spaces.

Hate speech, nationalistic tropes, nativist and racist slurs, uttered either in jest—for the sake of the lulz[27]—or to provoke intentionally, spread from the fringes of the Internet to occupy the center of public conversations. Trolling as a new genre of political speech, promoted by the virality and popularity incentives of social media, is becoming a salient trait of the new mediated public discourse. From a fringe political practice to now a mainstream form of political spectacle, trolling has become a staple of the political discussions enabled by social media (Marwick and Lewis 2017;

---

[27] *Lulz* is an alteration of the acronym LOL ('laughing out loud' or 'lots of laughs'), often used in on-line conversations.

Hannan 2018). The alt-right on-line communities and their media ecosystem, based on a plurality of platforms such as Breitbart News, Infowars, 4chan and Reddit, have received significant academic and media attention (Benkler et al. 2018; Marwick and Lewis 2017; Nagle 2017). In particular, the subcultural symbols, codes and jargons emerging out of on-line forums such as 4chan and Reddit seem to have had a profound impact in shaping the alt-right political sensibilities. Benkler et al. call the meme wars or 'memetic warfare' of the alt-right as a new type of 'core political speech' (Benkler et al. 2018, 12).

The alt-right community and its media have played a significant role in the advent of the post-truth condition. As pointed out by Bennett and Livingston, the term alt-right has expanded "to encompass a broader range of interconnected radical right causes and conspiracies theories promoted through information sites that often mimic journalism in order to distribute strategic disinformation" (Bennett and Livingston 2018, 125). Such alternative communication spaces often circulate political narratives advocating for 'stronger authority, nationalism and anti-immigration' policies, which often engender the 'disinformation–amplification–reverberation' cycle that allows them to enter the mainstream media and public discourse. While the focus of Bennet and Livingston is on the American political context, many other nations are currently suffering a similar problem. In their argument, the already discussed trust crisis in democratic institutions is linked to the hollowing out of mass parties and declining electoral representation. Such breakdown of essential processes of political representation and engagement makes "national information systems vulnerable to strategic disinformation campaigns by a plurality of actors" (Bennett and Livingston 2018, 127), both domestic and foreign.

A further dimension of post-truth discussed by this book is indeed the influence operations carried by State actors based on disinformation and media manipulation aimed at destabilizing elections and governments, or to influence the course of armed conflicts (Woolley and Howard 2018). Such strategic forms of computational propaganda are aimed at inserting false and polarizing information and narratives into the political conversations of other nations. Covert influence tactics operate by leveraging the technological features and affordances of social media, by taking advantage of the difficulty that lawmakers have in regulating and policing such platforms, as well as by tapping on popular sentiments of discontent and frustration to further exacerbate the political crisis of rival countries.

1.4   PLAN OF THE BOOK

In the coming chapters, the book will cover various case studies, each exploring one of the themes of the broader post-truth condition previously discussed. Chapter 2 will recount, analyze and theoretically frame the impact of influence operations carried by Russian trolls coordinated by the IRA to covertly influence the 2016 presidential elections in the United States. The chapter locates the IRA development in the context of domestic Russian politics and its later development as an agent of information warfare in the conflict in Ukraine. The chapter explores the theme of political polarization within American society, which was exploited and exacerbated by a coordinated strategy of political interference directed by the Kremlin aimed at sowing distrust and confusions among voters.

Chapter 3 discusses the circulation of conspiracy theories which evolve from concoctions of social media users or Internet subcultures to become global topics of public conversation and political mobilization, as well as tactical resources of influence operations by State actors. The examples provided are those of the Pizzagate and QAnon conspiracy theories, which embody the anti-establishment ethos, the paranoid disposition and the ironic attitude of alt-right communities. The chapter also analyzes the spreading of a set of myths, symbols and codes created by the 4chan and 8chan users within a global network of White ethnonationalists. The far-right anti-immigration conspiracy theory 'The Great Replacement' is discussed to explore the interlocking themes of ethnonationalist politics, White identity politics, trolling and the 'weaponization' of Internet entertainment.

Chapter 4 presents a case study based on the analysis of a disinformation campaign carried by the Syrian regime and its ally Russia via computational propaganda and so-called rumor bombs against the search and rescue organization globally known as the White Helmets, who operate since 2014 in Syria's rebel-held areas. This case study on the Syrian Civil War shows how rumors, conspiracy theories and other post-truth narratives in support of the Assad regime were exploited and given amplification by Russian media and via social media by a group of self-styled independent journalists and social media influencers, as well as by political bots and sock-puppet accounts. Such manipulative and propagandistic efforts found a receptive audience in Western countries, where social media users actively shared or co-created fictional narratives in a cultural and political context characterized by public opinion radicalization and polarization.

The disruptive impact of social media companies in politically volatile contexts in the Global South will be investigated in Chapter 5. The controversial role of Facebook in facilitating hate speech and disinformation that led to the ethnic cleansing of the Rohingya Muslim minority in Myanmar will be discussed.[28] The chapter will also analyze the role of Facebook subsidiary WhatsApp in allowing the circulation of disinformation during the 2018 general elections in Brazil, won by controversial far-right politician Jair Bolsonaro. The chapter argues that the role of private technology companies as arbiters of global political speech is often problematic, as their economic model and their incentives tend to favor sensational and inflammatory content. The problem is compounded by the inability of State institutions, particularly in countries with a weak democratic tradition, to exert control and enforce oversight on the content of social media platforms.

The conclusive Chapter 6 offers closing remarks on the geopolitical significance of the post-truth crisis, by drawing from the multiple case studies in the previous chapters. Examples are discussed that show possible avenues of technical, educational, regulatory and political intervention that can effectively curb the global spread of misinformation and disinformation, with the broader goal of restoring trust in mediating institutions and in the democratic process.

References

Appadurai, A. (1990). Disjuncture and difference in the global cultural economy. *Theory, Culture & Society, 7*(2–3), 295–310.

Arendt, H. (1972). *Crises of the republic.* New York, NY: Harcourt Brace Jovanovich.

Baym, G., & Jones, J. P. (2012). News parody in global perspective. *Popular Communication, 10*(1–2), 2–13.

Benkler, J., et al. (2018). *Network propaganda. Manipulation, disinformation, and radicalization in American politics.* Oxford: Oxford University Press.

Bennett, W. L., & Livingston, S. (2018). The disinformation order: Disruptive communication and the decline of democratic institutions. *European Journal of Communication, 33*(2), 122–139.

---

[28] Ellis-Petersen, H. (2018). "Facebook admits failings over incitement to violence in Myanmar". *The Guardian.* https://www.theguardian.com/technology/2018/nov/06/facebook-admits-it-has-not-done-enough-to-quell-hate-in-myanmar.

Berardi, F. (2017). Verità e simulazione. *Alfabeta2*. https://www.alfabeta2.it/2017/04/09/verita-e-simulazione.

Corner, J., & Pels, D. (2003). *Media and the restyling of politics: Consumerism, celebrity and cynicism*. London: Sage.

Cosentino, G. (2017). *L'era della post-verità: Media e populismi dalla Brexit a Trump*. Reggio Emilia: Imprimatur.

Cosentino, G., & Doyle, W. (2010). Silvio Berlusconi: The one-man brand. In M. Aronczyk & D. Powers (Eds.), *Blowing up the brand: Critical perspectives on promotional culture*. New York: Peter Lang.

D'Ancona, M. (2017). *Post-truth: The new war on truth and how to fight back*. London: Ebury Press.

Dean, J. (2010). The real internet. *International Journal of Zizek Studies, 4*(1), 1–22.

DiResta, D., et al. (2018). *The tactics & tropes of the internet research agency*. New Knowledge.

Farkas, J., & Schou, J. (2018). Fake news as a floating signifier: Hegemony, antagonism and the politics of falsehood. *Javnost: The Public, 25*(3), 298–314.

Foucault, M. (1976/2000). Truth and power. In J. D. Faubion (Ed.), *Power: Essential works of Foucault, 1954–1984* (Vol. 3, pp. 111–133). New York, NY: New Press.

Fukuyama, F. (1992). *The end of history and the last man*. New York: Free Press.

Habermas, J. (1991). *The structural transformations of the public sphere*. Cambridge: MIT Press.

Hannan, J. (2018). Trolling ourselves to death? Social media and post-truth politics. *European Journal of Communication, 33*(2), 214–226.

Harsin, J. (2015). Regimes of post truth, post politics, and attention economies. *Communication, Culture & Critique, 8*(2), 327–333.

Harsin, J. (2018). Post-truth and critical communication. In *Oxford research encyclopedia of communication*. Oxford: Oxford University Press. https://doi.org/10.1093/acrefore/9780190228613.013.757.

Harvey, D. (2005). *A brief history of neoliberalism*. Oxford: Oxford University Press.

Inglehart, R., & Norris, P. (2016). *Trump, Brexit, and the rise of Populism: Economic have-nots and cultural backlash* (Harvard Kennedy School Faculty Research Working Paper Series).

Judis, J. (2016). *The populist explosion*. New York: Columbia Global Reports.

Kakutani, M. (2018). *The death of truth*. New York: Tim Duggan Books.

Kalpokas, I. (2018). *A political theory of post-truth*. London: Palgrave Macmillan.

Kazin, M. (2016). Trump and American populism: Old whine, new bottles. *Foreign Affairs*. https://www.foreignaffairs.com/articles/united-states/2016-10-06/trump-and-american-populism.

Lyotard, J. (1984). *The postmodern condition: A report on knowledge*. Minneapolis: University of Minnesota Press.
Marwick, A., & Lewis, R. (2017). *Media manipulation and disinformation online*. Data and Society Research Institute.
Mattelart, A. (2002). An archaeology of the global era: Constructing a belief. *Media, Culture and Society, 24*(5), 591–612.
McIntyre, L. (2018). *Post-truth*. Cambridge: MIT Press.
McNair, B. (2008). *The internet and the changing global media environment*. In A. Chadwick & P. Howard (Eds.), *The Routledge handbook of internet politics* (pp. 217–229). London: Routledge.
Nagle, A. (2017). *Kill all normies*. Alresford: Zero Books.
Nichols, T. (2017). *The death of expertise*. Oxford: Oxford University Press.
Pariser, E. (2011). *The filter bubble: How the new personalized web is changing what we read and how we think*. New York: Penguin.
Pieterse, J. N. (2003). *Globalization and culture: Global mélange*. Lanham, MD: Rowman & Littlefield Publishers.
Pomerantsev, P., & Weiss M. (2014). *The menace of unreality: How the Kremlin weaponizes information, culture and money*. New York: The Interpreter.
Revelli, M. (2019). *La politica senza politica*. Torino: Einaudi.
Salgado, S. (2018). Online media impact on politics: Views on post-truth politics and post-postmodernism. *International Journal of Media & Cultural Politics, 14*(3), 317–331. https://doi.org/10.1386/macp.14.3.317_1.
Susca, V., & De Kerckhove, D. (2008). *Transpolitica. Nuovi rapporti di potere e sapere*. Milan: Apogeo.
Tuathail, G., et al. (2006). *The geopolitics reader*. London: Routledge.
Tufecki, Z. (2017). *Twitter and tear gas: The power and fragility of networked protest*. New Haven: Yale University Press.
Vaidhyanathan, S. (2018). *Anti-social media: How Facebook disconnects us and undermines democracy*. Oxford: Oxford University Press.
Van Herpen, M. (2016). *Putin's propaganda machine soft power and Russian foreign policy*. Lanham, MD: Rowman & Littlefield.
Waisbord, S. (2018). Why populism is troubling for democratic communication. *Communication Culture & Critique, 11*, 21–34.
Woolley, S., & Howard, P. (2018). *Computational propaganda*. Oxford: Oxford University Press.

CHAPTER 2

Polarize and Conquer: Russian Influence Operations in the United States

Abstract This chapter recounts, analyzes and theoretically frames the impact of influence operations carried by Russian trolls coordinated by the Internet Research Agency (IRA) to covertly influence the 2016 presidential elections in the United States. The chapter locates the IRA development in the context of domestic Russian politics and its later evolution as an agent of information warfare in the conflict in Ukraine. The chapter also discusses the theme of political polarization within American society, which was exploited and exacerbated by a coordinated strategy of political interference directed by the Kremlin aimed at sowing distrust and confusions among voters.

Keywords Trolling · Internet Research Agency (IRA) · Russia · Hybrid warfare · Facebook

2.1 INTRODUCTION

The chapter discusses the influence operations[1] carried by the Kremlin-affiliated on-line propaganda outfit known as the Internet Research

---

[1] "Information operations and warfare, also known as influence operations, include the collection of tactical information about an adversary as well as the dissemination of propaganda in pursuit of a competitive advantage over an opponent". See https://www.rand.org/topics/information-operations.html.

© The Author(s) 2020
G. Cosentino, *Social Media and the Post-Truth World Order*,
https://doi.org/10.1007/978-3-030-43005-4_2

Agency (IRA), which covertly interfered with the 2016 US presidential elections. The influence strategy is discussed with reference to Russian politics by looking at the IRA as a hub of information warfare in support of the Russian government, both for national issues and in the context of the military intervention in Ukraine. Special emphasis in the analysis is given to the concept of 'managed democracy,' a form of government hiding an autocratic core behind a façade of democratic procedures and institutions. The term is discussed in the chapter as an ideological precursor to the media manipulation efforts carried by Russia in the United States.

The case study presented in support of the analysis discusses a series of political events in the United States organized via social media by the IRA with the unwitting cooperation of real American activists. The IRA operations are observed as a revealing example of contemporary Russian propaganda strategies, based on the 'weaponization of information' (Pomerantsev and Weiss 2014). Such influence strategy is discussed through the theoretical prism of post-truth politics, particularly with reference to the trust crisis in political and cultural institutions and to postmodern ideological relativism.

The chapter also explores the growing cultural and political divisions within American society. The epistemic crisis, the decline in authority of democratic institutions and ideological polarization at the heart of the post-truth condition were exploited by the influence operations by a hostile foreign actor. The chapter also demonstrates how Russia is exploiting the post-truth condition within Western democracies to challenge their global supremacy and advance its geopolitical agenda.

2.2   This Is What Managed Democracy Looks Like

On Saturday May 21, 2016, two small crowds of demonstrators squared off at noon in front of the Da'Wah Islamic Center in Houston, Texas. One protest had been assembled by the *Heart of Texas* Facebook group, which boasted the headline 'Texas: homeland of guns, BBQ and ur heart' and presented itself as an organization in favor of the secession of Texas from the United States. The Facebook group, which at the time counted over 250,000 followers, had created the event 'Stop the Islamization of

Texas,' and the roughly fifty people that attended waved confederate flags, chanted anti-Muslim slogans and wore 'White Lives Matter' t-shirts. On the other side of the street, a completely different crowd of counter-protesters, slightly outnumbering their opponents, attended the event 'Save Islamic Knowledge' that had been organized on the same day and location by another Facebook group, *United Muslims of America*, which counted more than 300,000 followers. These demonstrators carried signs against Islamophobia, waved 'Antifa' symbols and unrolled a large black banner with an illustration of Hitler pointing a gun to his head. *Follow your leader, kill yourself*, read the slogan on the banner.

Six months later, on November 12, 10,000 people gathered in New York City's Union Square to protest the election of Donald Trump to the presidency of the United States. They were attending the 'Trump is NOT my president. March against Trump' event, organized by the Facebook group *BlackMattersUS*, which presented itself as a community of activists with a mission "to tell the bold truth about racism, inequality and injustice the mainstream media keep out-of-sight." The description of the event, which was shared on Facebook with 61,000 people, read: "Divided is the reason we just fell. We must unite despite our differences to stop HATE from ruling the land." It was the most widely attended of the many demonstrations that took place across America in the immediate aftermath of the 2016 election. The vast crowd marched for over forty blocks, until it reached the Trump Tower, carrying signs against racism, sexism, homophobia and chanting "This is what democracy looks like!".

At first sight, the street confrontation in Houston on an issue as sensitive as Muslim immigration in the post-9/11 America and the wave of popular discontent in New York against Trump's election might have appeared as genuine displays of American grassroots activism, signaling a robust tradition of political participation which flares up in periods of contentious politics. But upon closer scrutiny, there was a catch, which was revealed one year later by the US Senate Select Committee on Intelligence investigating Russian interference in the 2016 US elections. None of the organizers actually showed up to the rallies, since the events, as well as the Facebook groups behind them, had been created by a shadowy agency based in St. Petersburg, Russia, known as the Internet Research Agency, or IRA.

In its on-line propaganda campaigns, carried between 2013 and 2018, the IRA—which US officials defined as a 'troll farm'—operated like a sophisticated digital marketing agency, employing over a thousand people to perform round the clock influence operations in various world regions. In the United States, the operations started around 2014 and continued through 2018.[2] The IRA was founded and financed by Yevgeny Prigozhin, a Russian oligarch in the food catering business with close ties to Russian President Vladimir Putin and to Russian intelligence.[3] In February 2018, Prigozhin was among the several Russian citizens and entities indicted by the US Justice Department Special Counsel Robert Mueller, who was investigating Russian information warfare against the United States and possible collusions between the Trump campaign[4] and the Russian government.[5] The IRA was also among the entities indicted with charges of conspiracy to defraud the United States by unlawfully interfering in its political and electoral process through a series of influence operations that were described as 'information warfare.'[6]

[2] The data provided by the major technology companies to the US Senate Select Committee on Intelligence "illustrate that for approximately five years, Russia has waged a propaganda war against American citizens, manipulating social media narratives to influence American culture and politics". DiResta, D., et al. (2018). *The tactics & tropes of the internet research agency* (p. 6). New Knowledge.

[3] Eltagouri, M. (2018). "The rise of 'Putin's chef,' the Russian oligarch accused of manipulating the U.S. election". *Washington Post.* https://beta.washingtonpost.com/news/worldviews/wp/2018/02/16/the-rise-of-putins-chef-yevgeniy-prigozhin-the-russian-accused-of-manipulating-the-u-s-election/?noredirect=on.

[4] "The IRA had a very clear bias for then-candidate Trump's that spanned from early in the campaign and throughout the data set. A substantial portion of political content articulated pro-Donald Trump sentiments, beginning with the early primaries" (DiResta et al. 2018, 9).

[5] While the Mueller report fell short of accusing President Trump of collusion with Russian agents, it nonetheless concluded that "the Russian government interfered in the 2016 presidential election in sweeping and systematic fashion". See Editorial Board. (2019). "The Mueller report and the danger facing American democracy". *The New York Times.* https://www.nytimes.com/2019/04/19/opinion/mueller-report-trump-russia.html.

[6] "Information warfare can cover a vast range of different activities and processes seeking to steal, plant, interdict, manipulate, distort or destroy information. The channels and methods available for doing this cover an equally broad range, including computers, smartphones, real or invented news media, statements by leaders or celebrities, online troll campaigns, text messages, vox pops by concerned citizens, YouTube videos, or direct approaches to individual human targets. Recent Russian campaigning provides examples of all of the above and more". Giles, K. (2016). *Handbook of Russian information warfare* (p. 4). Nato Defense College.

The Special Counsel indictments confirmed what had already been reported first by Buzzfeed in 2014,[7] by *The New York Times* in 2015[8] and by several other later reports on the operations and the structure of on-line propaganda outfits affiliated with the Kremlin. The indictments laid bare the multiple disinformation tactics employed by the IRA to influence American politics, including disseminating false information on the pres-idential candidates, particularly Hillary Clinton,[9] and impersonating the role of activists in order to mobilize American citizens around a plurality of divisive issues.

What had been initially discussed and analyzed by journalists and scholars (Seddon 2014; Chen 2015; Confessore & Wakabayashi 2017; Vaidhyanathan 2018) was thus officially condemned by the American judiciary: Russia leveraged popular social media platforms such as Face-book, Instagram, Twitter and YouTube to wage an information warfare against the United States. A campaign of disinformation that had started with an hoax about a fake terrorist attack on US ground (Chen 2015) later evolved into a machinery, at times amateurish at others very effec-tive, geared toward pitting American political communities against each other by means of incendiary memes and fabricated events disseminated via social media. The operations of the IRA are part of a broader Russian state-run soft power and propaganda apparatus that includes the multilin-gual all-news network RT, the on-line news agency Sputnik, think tanks, foundations and social and religious groups, which often cooperate in order to amplify pro-Kremlin political narratives.

According to a report compiled by cybersecurity company New Knowl-edge in collaboration with Columbia University, the disinformation cam-paign leading up to the 2016 US elections was part of a three-pronged strategy which also included the attempted hacking of the voting system, the cyberattack of the Democratic National Committee email server, with the subsequent release of a trove of confidential emails to the alternative

---

[7] Seddon, M. (2014). "Documents show how Russia's troll army hit America". *Buzzfeed.* https://www.buzzfeednews.com/article/maxseddon/documents-show-how-russias-troll-army-hit-america.

[8] Chen, A. (2015). "The agency. An investigation into the Russian troll farm called the Internet Research Agency". *The New York Times Magazine.* https://www.nytimes.com/2015/06/07/magazine/the-agency.html.

[9] "A substantial portion of political content articulated anti-Hillary Clinton sentiments among both Right and Left-leaning IRA-created communities" (DiResta et al. 2018, 9).

information site WikiLeaks—which provided inspiration for the so-called *Pizzagate* conspiracy theory discussed in Chapter 3—and also a vast and sustained operation "designed to exert political influence and exacerbate social divisions in US culture."[10]

Facing mounting political pressure and public scrutiny, technology companies such as Facebook, Twitter and Google have provided the Senate Committee with data sets indicating, albeit incompletely,[11] the breadth of the various activities conducted by the IRA to spread manipulative content. The broader goal of these media manipulation tactics through fictitious personas via social media was to influence the outcome of the 2016 elections in support of Trump, while simultaneously polarizing a society increasingly fractured along ideological fault-lines.

Public opinion polarization[12] has been discussed extensively as one of the defining features of the current age of political communications via social media, a condition that scholars link to the spread of disinformation and to negative effects on the democratic process (Tucker et al. 2018). Closeted social groupings of like-minded citizens increasingly exist and operate in the form 'filter bubbles' algorithmically engendered by social media and search engines (Pariser 2011). In the United States, the Internet has allowed for a further splintering of a public opinion which since at least three decades has been divided in opposing ideological fronts by broadcast media such as talk radio and all-news television networks (Cosentino 2017). Identity politics challenging established political traditions and institutions, as well as so-called culture wars across cultural, religious, ethnic and geographic cleavages were also important preconditions of the growing ideological and affective political polarization among American citizens. Studies also have indicated a link between political polarization over social media and the circulation of both propaganda, malicious disinformation and unintentional misinformation. Tucker et al. (2018) suggest that political polarization and disinformation might be

---

[10] Ibid., 4.

[11] The New Knowledge reports lament that "none of the platforms (Twitter, Facebook, and Alphabet) appears to have turned over complete sets. (...) Each lacked core components that would have provided a fuller and more actionable picture" (DiResta et al. 2018, 5).

[12] The concept indicates the extent to which supporters of a political party dislike the competing political party and its supporters.

fueling each other, while also stressing the importance of preexisting political engagement in this process. A well-known 2016 Buzzfeed report[13] suggested a connection between the circulation of disinformation and engagement levels among social media users, particularly those active in hyper-partisan group both from the alt-right and from the far-left ecosystems.

Russian trolls at the IRA didn't simply fabricate incendiary material or events via social media, but rather exploited and further amplified already existing grievances within American society. As argued by Confessore and Wakabayashi (2017), they manipulated the "the anger, passion and misinformation" that Americans were already expressing and sharing via social media. As part of their broader influence strategy, IRA trolls created a plurality of Facebook groups, such as the already mentioned *Heart of Texas* or *BlackMattersUS*, which would mimic the rhetoric and content of real hyper-partisan groups, with the goal of disseminating sensational and polarizing content, in some cases patently false, often taken or rehashed from real American sources on mainstream or social media.

As previously discussed, the spread of disinformation is linked to legitimacy problems of the main institutions of contemporary liberal democracies, one of the primary features of the post-truth condition, which lends itself to the exploitation by hostile foreign State actors. As argued by Bennett and Livingston (2018), propaganda efforts by foreign agents leverage on the "ennui and anger that accompanies the hollowing out of mainstream institutions of the state and society." This statement suggests a precise strategy on the part of foreign countries, in this case Russia, based on preying upon the inherent fragilities of Western democracies, especially of their traditional rival, the United States. Scholars and researchers (DiResta et al. 2018) agree that the IRA goal was to further stoke and spread confusion and distrust among American citizens on structural issues within their societies, in their democratic system and in their political establishment.

By artificially amplifying divisions in the American electorate, Russian agents applied a media manipulation strategy similar to the one that had been employed domestically since the early days of the Putin's presidency. Such strategy was part of a political philosophy that went by the name

---

[13] Silverman, C., et al. (2016). "Hyperpartisan Facebook pages are publishing false and misleading information at an alarming rate". *Buzzfeed*. https://www.buzzfeed.com/craigsilverman/partisan-fb-pages-analysis?utm_term=.jnB0mGP48x#.toaL7DxX3l.

of 'managed democracy,' defining a government constituted formally as democratic, which, however, functions as a de facto autocracy (Snyder 2018).

To understand the roots of this strategy, one needs to appreciate the influence exerted on Russian politics during the early 2000s by former Deputy Chief of Staff Vladislav Surkov, the 'political technologist' credited with popularizing the notion of managed democracy (Pomerantsev 2014a; Snyder 2018). In the Adam Curtis 2016 documentary *Hypernormalization*, Surkov is mentioned as one of the people who better understood how uncertainty about the future and lack of belief in politics and institutions, which followed the collapse of the Soviet Union and the dramatic transition to democracy under Boris Eltsin, could be exploited to bolster a new type of power, an hybrid between democracy and dictatorship, which would then become embodied by the three presidencies of Vladimir Putin.

Among the political technologists of twenty-first-century Russia, Surkov stood out as the one with the most radical vision, drawn from his education in the theater arts, his passion for literature and pop culture and his career in the advertising and PR business for one of Russia's largest banks. Under Surkov supervision as Putin's chief ideologist, politics was turned into a "theatre where nobody knew what was true and what was fake any longer" (Curtis 2016). Surkov's aim was not simply to manipulate people, but to undermine their very grasp and perception of reality. Surkov, further observes Curtis, turned Russian politics into "a constantly changing piece of theatre," simultaneously sponsoring imitation political parties and fake social movements, consisting of both nationalist skinheads and pro-Kremlin youth groups on the one hand, and human rights groups on the other, and encouraging their confrontation to simulate a thriving democracy and to spread unrest and confusion among the public opinion. In Surkov's own words: "If you criticize democracy in Russia, then that means it exists. If there are demonstrations, it means there is democracy. They don't have demonstrations in totalitarian states."[14] It was a strategy that according to Pomerantsev (2011) was meant to keep

[14] Sawka, R. (2011). "Surkov: Dark prince of the Kremlin". *Open Democracy*. https://www.opendemocracy.net/od-russia/richard-sakwa/surkov-dark-prince-of-kremlin.

opposition confused[15] and "to own all forms of political discourse, to not let any independent movements develop outside of its walls."[16]

Meanwhile, the real power in Putin's Russia—the corporate takeover of national resources, the consolidation of the media into government-friendly ownership, the raiding of private companies by powerful and corrupt oligarchs, the murdering of dissenting voices in politics and in the press[17]—was hidden from the political stage and exercised without significant public scrutiny and accountability. Democracy thus was apparently functioning, with elections being held regularly and street demonstrations happening among the different political currents, but its core of representation of people's interests had been stripped out of any meaningful substance. Surkov helped to create "a world of masks and poses, colorful but empty, with little at its core but power for power's sake and the accumulation of vast wealth."[18] This is the managed democracy that, according to observers such as Pomerantsev, Russia has been experiencing under Putin since then early 2000s.

Confusion was thus used as a system of political control that Surkov built on Western cultural references, such as the postmodern ideas popularized by French scholars like Lyotard on the breakdown of grand cultural narratives and on the fragmentation of truth, discussed in the previous chapter as the historical and philosophical precondition to the current post-truth era. According to Dixon (2016), a correspondence has been noted between Surkov's approach to politics and the theories of Lyotard on the postmodern condition, characterized by multiple perspectives and micro-narratives in lieu of grand totalizing truths. According to Pomerantsev (2011), a postmodern sensibility was at the heart of Surkov idea of

---

[15] Pomerantsev, P. (2011). "Putin's Rasputin". *London Review of Books*. https://www.lrb.co.uk/v33/n20/peter-pomerantsev/putins-rasputin.

[16] Pomerantsev, P. (2014a). "The hidden author of Putinism. How Vladislav Surkov invented the new Russia". *The Atlantic*. https://www.theatlantic.com/international/archive/2014/11/hidden-author-putinism-russia-vladislav-surkov/382489/.

[17] With respect to this, Roudakova (2017) observes that "With the arrival of President Putin in 2000, press freedom was further and unequivocally curtailed as private media began to be harassed, censorship was reintroduced, and independent journalists began to be threatened and even murdered" (p. 3).

[18] Pomerantsev (2011).

managed democracy: "Russia has adopted a fashionable, supposedly liber-ational Western intellectual movement and transformed it into an instrument of oppression." One could thus argue that Russia has pioneered the style of political management that characterizes contemporary populist leaders such as Trump, who seems to thrive in a post-truth scenario where objective truth, empirical evidence and truth-arbitering institutions have lost their preeminence in public discourses.

The point of the Surkovian approach to politics, which predates the global onset of post-truth, is not to push for a certain well-rounded propagandistic narrative, as it was standard practice during the Soviet era, but rather to disseminate a plurality of conflicting narratives, partly real and party fictional, and to question people's ability to tell the real from the fictional, and the true from the false. Roudakova, in her thorough study of the decline of journalism in contemporary Russia, also emphasizes the difference between Soviet propaganda and the brand of propaganda under Putin, stigmatizing the 'defactualization' of reality it produces: "To contemporary propagandists the notion of factual accuracy has become superfluous. (...) The goal of the new propaganda is not to persuade anyone but to confuse and distract, spawning ever more grotesque interpretations of reality and spreading distrust in any and all truth claims" (Roudakova 2017, 218).

In contemporary Russia, political reality has thus been reinvented in a form of a 'mass hallucination' that can be altered to take any shape, while simultaneously maintaining its fundamental core of power balances unchallenged and unaltered. According to Dixon, Surkov "through his frank dissemination of ambiguous and contradictory statements, fiction, humor, honesty, heresy (...) swamps any existing narrative, defamiliarising the entire landscape and in the process undermining trust in any existing information structure."[19] This last point echoes the observations raised by D'Ancona (2017) and Harsin (2018), mentioned in the introduction, who consider a crisis of trust in journalism and the media as foundational of the post-truth condition. Quoting again Roudakova (2017, 220): "As facts are reduced to opinions and opinions masquerade as facts, boundaries between fact, opinion, and fabrication disappear, and with them disappears the stability of a shared reality."

---

[19] Dixon, J. (2016). "Is Vladislav Surkov an artist?" *New Minds Eye*. https://newmindseye.wordpress.com/is-vladislav-surkov-an-artist/.

The IRA dissemination of false information and the creation of fake groups of activists during the 2016 US elections appear to follow the same dystopian vision of democracy concocted by Surkov: a vision that exacerbates the inherent flaws, divisions and issues within American politics and society to further tear the population apart, bewilder and confuse the public opinion, disable genuine opposition and bolster the rise of leaders and power brokers with demagogic and autocratic tendencies such as Donald Trump. In order to better understand how the IRA fits within the broader Russian political context and contemporary history, it is worth recounting its development and its later employment as a key component of Russia's new aggressive foreign policy.

2.3   The IRA's 'Non-linear' Information Warfare

The IRA was created to mimic the model of the Chinese on-line propaganda outfits such as the 50 Cent Army, who closely monitor and manage public opinion on the Internet (Woolley & Howard 2018). Its establishment, which is believed to be dated to 2013, was part of a two-pronged strategy employed by Russia after 2011 to rein in the politically disruptive effects on domestic politics of new communication technologies, particularly social media. On the one hand, draconian laws on blogs were enacted and major national social media such as VKontakte were forcibly placed under the ownership of government-friendly companies, in order to stifle the growth of a free and independent public sphere on-line. On the other hand, propaganda and manipulation strategies via social media were devised and implemented to influence both the national and the international public opinion, particularly in the United States, with the goal of creating polarization on key political issues. "Control at home and dissent and unrest abroad" was the grand strategy, as summed up by the original Buzzfeed report on Kremlin-affiliated trolls (Seddon 2014).

The application to the Internet of the strategy for public opinion control and manipulation that eventually paved the way for the IRA was developed under the supervision of Vyacheslav Volodin, 10th Chairman of the State Duma. Volodin has been credited for engineering Putin conservative turn after 2012, for his third term as Russian President, during which a resurgence of traditional and religious values was promoted and a Eurasian geopolitical view with Russia at its helm was crafted by a number of ideologues and conservative thinkers, including notorious far-right philosopher Alexandr Dugin (Engström 2014). At the time, many middle-class Russians who had come of age during the more liberal decades of the early 2000s protested against alleged frauds during Putin's elections for a third term and against corruption among the ruling elites, with many of the rallies being organized through social media and blogs.

Some commentators speculate (Milam 2018) that Surkov's strategy to engineer and manipulate dissent had backfired around 2011–2012, as social media and blogs gave an unexpected and genuine boost to Russian opposition parties and civil society groups. While most of the Kremlin attention during the early 2000s was on controlling broadcast media, especially television, up until 2012 the Internet had been left relatively free from political interference, allowing for a thriving blogosphere to develop (Sanovich in Woolley and Howard 2018). Volodin was chosen as a replacement to Vladislav Surkov after the greatest wave of protests that had been seen in Russia since the 1990s. Volodin adopted Surkov playbook for polarizing and manipulating the public opinion, while, however, making sure that political divisions wouldn't escalate into actual activity on the ground.

The ultimate goal of the new strategy was to turn the Internet into an unreliable source of information, by polluting the on-line conversations with false information, presenting contradicting versions of events and pitting different sections of the public opinion against each other. This manipulative approach to social media, which served as the rationale for the creation of troll farms such as IRA, was first tested on domestic issues to disable the 2011–2021 wave of protests—attacking popular opposition figures such as Alexei Navalny and Boris Nemtsov[20]—and then eventually applied to other contexts, like Ukraine, the Baltic states, Eastern Europe, the Middle East and eventually the United States.

Under Putin's third term, an important political evolution was what Pomerantsev calls 'perpetual war mobilization', which resurrected old imperial ambitions as well as Soviet-era fears of a Western threat. In practice, it translated into stoking anxieties about Western encroachment into countries neighboring Russia, which could be used to justify retaliatory

---

[20] When Nemtsov was killed in 2015, the IRA trolls received several assignments in order to instill doubts and confusion around his death, pushing forward several narratives meant at shifting the blame from the Kremlin to Nemtsov's friends or on Ukrainian oligarchs. See Parfitt, T. (2015). "My life as a pro-Putin propagandist in Russia's secret 'troll factory'". *The Telegraph*. https://www.telegraph.co.uk/news/worldnews/europe/russia/11656043/My-life-as-a-pro-Putin-propagandist-in-Russias-secret-troll-factory.html.

or even preemptive military actions. Such nationalist warmongering was applied expediently to quell the unrest and internal divisions surfacing in 2011, and to consolidate Putin's power after his controversial 2012 third election as president. Russian domestic and foreign policy strategies—which combined propaganda against foreign countries via broadcast media and the Internet, lavish soft power initiatives such as the 2012 Sochi Winter Games and the 2018 FIFA World Cup, and reinvigorated nationalism with a religious and messianic streak—were at times underestimated or even misunderstood as being backwards, particularly by the Obama administration. In reality, the Kremlin "acted as a geopolitical *avant-garde*, informed by a dark, subversive reading of globalization" (Pomerantsev 2014a) whereby old geopolitical paradigms were upended by flows of capitals, people and cultural or political symbols that challenged both State borders and postwar Atlanticist alliances like the EU or NATO.[21] This is the foreign policy vision that Russia increasingly put forth in the lead-up to and following the 2014 annexation of Crimea, formerly part of Ukraine.

Disinformation and propaganda were key components of Russian military campaign in Ukraine. Some of the examples of Russian disinformation in the conflict have become well-known examples in the tradition of information warfare: one Russian current-affairs program featured an actor posing in the same segment first as an anti-Russian and later as a pro-Russian activist,[22] and during a news program a woman falsely accused Ukrainian nationalists of crucifying a child in the eastern Ukrainian city of Sloviansk.[23] Another sadly famous example is the downing of the MH17 passenger airplane flying over the Donbass region of Eastern Ukraine in

---

[21] Interestingly, when on March 17, 2014, President Obama banned Surkov from entering the United States in retaliation to the Russia annexation of Crimea, he responded by saying: "The only things that interest me in the US are Tupac Shakur, Allen Ginsberg, and Jackson Pollock. I don't need a visa to access their work".

[22] BBC News. (2014). "Russia TV stations air 'impostor' protester in two guises". *BBC*. https://www.bbc.com/news/blogs-news-from-elsewhere-26986657.

[23] Nemtsova, A. (2014). "There's no evidence the Ukrainian army crucified a child in Slovyansk". *The Daily Beast*. https://www.thedailybeast.com/theres-no-evidence-the-ukrainian-army-crucified-a-child-in-slovyansk.

July 2014, which killed 298 people between passengers and crew members. Official investigations have concluded that the plane was hit by anti-aircraft missiles in possession of pro-Russia separatist militias,[24] but in the aftermath of the crash the Russian media swiftly started to spread a variety of possible explanations aimed at absolving the rebels.[25]

The aim of the Russian media blitz on the MH17 was to distract people from the evidence that was being gathered in the aftermath of the crash, which was pointing to the separatists as culprits. However, rather than trying to convince people of one particular version of events, Russian media rushed to produce as many competing narratives as possible so as to leave the public opinion flabbergasted and unable to neither conduct a rational search for the truth nor form an evidence-based opinion. Challenged on the veracity of the reports, the Russian Deputy Minister of Information at the time cynically claimed that the fabricated reports were actually a boost to television ratings, as if the point of such blatant propaganda was not so much to persuade anyone, but to keep the viewer hooked and distracted, and to disrupt Ukrainian or Western narratives rather than providing a coherent counternarrative.

After its successful propaganda effort in support of the military campaign in Ukraine, the IRA was later appointed to become an essential part of the new Russian foreign policy. The use of social media to wage information warfare in foreign countries, including the United States, was in fact perfected by Russia during the war in Ukraine. It should be noted that IRA's attempts to influence the American public opinion date back to 2014, particularly within the context of the conflict in the Donbass. The goal was to challenge the condemning position of the Obama administration on Russia's annexation of Crimea and other Russian military operations in Ukraine, by posting in the comment sections of the major US on-line news outlets such as Fox News, Politico and the Huffington Post (Seddon 2014). It should be pointed out that, after his demotion as Deputy Chief of Staff, Surkov was appointed as Putin's aide on foreign

[24] Walker, S. (2018). "MH17 downed by Russian military missile system, say investigators". *The Guardian*. https://www.theguardian.com/world/2018/may/24/mh17-downed-by-russian-military-missile-system-say-investigators.

[25] Among the increasingly ludicrous hypotheses, the most notorious claimed that data from radars showed Ukrainian jets flying near the MH17 plane, suggesting that the plane was shot down by the Ukrainian army aiming at Mr. Putin's presidential jet, and that corpses unrelated to the event had been moved by the CIA to the plane crashing site to increase the death toll.

policy, with Ukraine in his portfolio.[26] In this new position, he was able to further pursue his model of theatrical political consultancy on a much more ambitious scale. In Ukraine, Surkov managed the image and communications of the separatist groups and helped stage a highly contested referendum that was used as a justification for the annexation of Crimea.

Surkov rightly understood that the 'weaponized relativism',[27] or the obfuscation of truth by a plurality of conflicting media narratives that he had perfected in Russian domestic politics, would resonate well in a Western world still recovering from the post-Iraq debacle and by the 2008 financial crisis, and increasingly suspicious of its own political and cultural institutions, where "reality-based discourse has already fractured into political partisanship."[28] In other words, a Western world that was gradually slipping into the post-truth condition. The managed democracy doctrine for domestic politics evolved into what Surkov, through his literary alter-ego Nathan Dubovitsky,[29] called the 'non-linear war,' a futuristic view of warfare whereby conflicts happen between multiple fronts with shifting alliances, and whose ultimate goal is not necessarily military success but rather a process of constant disorientation and destabilization that could be exploited for geopolitical ends.

The Kremlin's 'non-linear' approach to foreign policy thus relies on an array of seemingly contradictory messages aimed at building alliances with ideologically different groups within Western democracies: European right-wing nationalists and populists such as Hungary's Jobbik, Italy's Lega Nord and Five Star Movement, or France's Front National rally around Russia's anti-EU message; American and European far-right and far-left sympathizers are attracted by the idea of Russia fighting American

[26] While the Kremlin has always denied his involvement in the military conflict in the Donbass region, a hacking of Surkov's email outed him as the de facto commander of pro-Russia separatists. See Embury-Dennis, T. (2016). "Russia's involvement in Ukraine conflict 'revealed after hackers' leak emails linked to Vladimir Putin's top aide". *The Independent*. https://www.independent.co.uk/news/world/europe/russia-ukraine-involvement-emails-hack-vladimir-putin-top-aide-crimea-war-a7397446.html.

[27] Storey, P. (2015). "Vladislav Surkov: The (gray) cardinal of the Kremlin". *Cicero Magazine*. http://ciceromagazine.com/features/the-gray-cardinal-of-the-kremlin/.

[28] Pomerantsev, P. (2014b). "Russia's ideology: There is no truth". *The New York Times*. https://www.nytimes.com/2014/12/12/opinion/russias-ideology-there-is-no-truth.html.

[29] See http://www.bewilderingstories.com/issue582/without_sky.html.

imperialism in Ukraine or in the Middle East; American religious conservatives appreciate Kremlin's religious revivalism and its position against homosexuality. Such contradictory messages appeal to Western audiences from multiple ideological perspectives and end up producing widespread political support for Russia.[30]

2.4   Fabricated Facebook Events in America

According to Surkov "all democracies are managed democracies,"[31] and political success is to be achieved by influencing people and by giving them the illusion of freedom. This cynical statement of political philosophy could be seen as the guiding logic behind the IRA strategy in the US elections: staging events that would give people a fake sense of freedom and participation, titillating their political inclinations with 'bait' content, polluting the media with multiple conflicting narratives, often fictitious, so as to make consensus impossible, and then operate to assist the victory of the most politically convenient candidate. According to Kakutani, the same 'Surkovian manipulation' that had shaped contemporary Russian politics also "informed Russian efforts to disrupt the 2016 U.S. election by impersonating Americans and grassroots political groups on social media" (Kakutani 2018, 241).

This section focuses on a number of events, organized via Facebook by the IRA, which happened on the US territory. According to the already mentioned indictments by the US Justice Department,[32] people working at IRA "took extraordinary steps to appear as ordinary American activists" on social media in order to reach out to real activists and citizens. Since 2014, by closely monitoring American politics[33] and focusing on the media ecosystems at the far-right and far-left fringes of the public opinion, Russian agents knew which topics to push. According to a Senator of

[30] Pomerantsev, P. (2014c). "How Putin is reinventing warfare". *Foreign Policy*. https://foreignpolicy.com/2014/05/05/how-putin-is-reinventing-warfare/.

[31] Sawka (2011).

[32] USA vs IRA et al. (2018). See https://www.justice.gov/file/1035477/download.

[33] According to a former IRA employee, IRA trolls were required to watch the well-known tv series *House of Cards* to learn about American politics. See Yahoo! News. (2017). "Russian trolls were schooled on 'House of Cards'". *Yahoo!* https://www.yahoo.com/news/russian-trolls-schooled-house-cards-185648522.html.

the Intelligence Committee, Russian operatives "spent months developing networks of real people to follow and like their content" which were later "utilized to push an array of disinformation."[34] Starting in 2014, the IRA began to monitor social media sites devoted to American politics and social issues by tracking "certain metrics like the group's size, the frequency of content placed by the group, and the level of audience engagement with that content, such as the average number of comments or responses to a post."[35] IRA operatives also travelled to the United States and contacted American political and social activists in order to gather intelligence on how to effectively interfere with the course of the elections. They also invested considerable resources in creating fictitious personas through social media and in turning them into influencers or public opinion leaders in the United States. The stated goal, as claimed by the indictments, was to elevate the intensity of US politics "through supporting radical groups, users dissatisfied with [the] social and economic situation and oppositional social movements."[36]

The IRA organized nearly 120 events across the United States via Facebook between 2015 and 2017, which were seen by over 300,000 people,[37] in some cases with a high attendance, and in other cases resulting in low turnout or in being uncovered by real activists.[38] The strategy was to identify hot-button issues and then mobilize citizens from both sides of the political spectrum. On the issue of race and police brutality, for example, the IRA-managed *Blue Lives Matter* counter-protest was held in Dallas in July 2016 across the street from where a legitimate Black Lives Matter protest rally was taking place. Also, *BlackMattersUS*, an IRA-run Facebook group, recruited unwitting local activists to organize a rally that was held in Charlotte, North Carolina, in 2016, protesting the shooting

---

[34] Abeshouse, B. (2018). "Facebook, Russian trolls and the new era of information warfare". *Al Jazeera*. https://www.aljazeera.com/blogs/americas/2018/01/facebook-russian-trolls-era-information-warfare-180131135425603.html.

[35] USA vs IRA et al. (2018, 12).

[36] Ibid., 14.

[37] O'Sullivan, D. (2018). "Russian trolls created Facebook events seen by more than 300,000 users". *CNN Money*. https://money.cnn.com/2018/01/26/media/russia-trolls-facebook-events/index.html.

[38] The IRA operations were not always successful, and real activists could not always be unwillingly coopted. What made some American citizens suspicious were the frequent grammatical mistakes in the communications by Russians and some imprecisions in organizing the events.

of an African-American by the police. On the issue of the 2016 presidential race, one event in support of Hillary Clinton and one against her were organized, respectively, in Washington and New York. In Florida, which was a key battleground for the 2016 election, several rallies dubbed 'Florida Goes Trump' were organized by the IRA in coordination with members of the official Trump campaign, which were allegedly unaware of cooperating with Russian agents.[39]

Over a hundred Facebook groups with partisan-sounding names like *Blacktivist, Being Patriotic, LGBT United* were all set up by the IRA to spread ideologically oriented content. Some examples were playing with a kind of millennials' cool irony, like a post promoting a Bernie Sanders coloring book. Others were aiming for a more tangible effect on people's life, like the organization of a self-defense group with a political slant for African-Americans called *Black Fist*, which was set up in New York City by the IRA via social media by recruiting experienced martial arts trainers and by promoting the classes with Facebook ads targeting black communities.[40] Within the broader strategy of leveraging ethnic or sociocultural cleavages within American society, the already mentioned New Knowledge report suggests that the IRA conducted long and extensive influence operations targeting African-American communities, with the goal of developing audiences and recruiting assets.[41]

Overall, by Facebook own admission in front of the Intelligence Committee, nearly 130 million Americans were exposed to the manipulative content circulated on the social network by agents of Russian disinformation. The content, spread by fake accounts, consisted of memes, events or other types of post with high virality potential for so-called organic

---

[39] In one of these events, an American citizen was paid to impersonate Hillary Clinton dressed in a prison uniform standing in a cage built on a flatbed truck.

[40] Adams, R., & Brown, H. (2017). "These Americans were tricked into working for Russia. They say they had no idea". *Buzzfeed News*. https://www.buzzfeednews.com/article/rosalindadams/these-americans-were-tricked-into-working-for-russia-they#.rgyD61X0Q.

[41] "The most prolific IRA efforts on Facebook and Instagram specifically targeted Black American communities and appear to have been focused on developing Black audiences and recruiting Black Americans as assets. The IRA created an expansive cross-platform media mirage targeting the Black community, which shared and cross-promoted authentic Black media to create an immersive influence ecosystem" (DiResta et al. 2018, 8).

reach,[42] as well as ads and promoted content on a plurality of political themes.[43] Overall, Russia invested nearly $100,000 in 2016 on 3000 Facebook ads on controversial issues with the goal of influencing both online and off-line political conversations across the ideological spectrum, while the broader IRA budget is estimated at an average $15 million per year.[44]

The public opinion manipulation efforts by the IRA exposed by the US Senate Select Committee on Intelligence revealed the level of sophistication reached by the information warfare strategies employed by Russia, from the hacking of the DNC mail servers to the spreading of disinformation via automated bot accounts on social media, from the polarization of the public opinion to the creation of divisive events. Such strategy seems to replicate Russia's postmodern approach to authoritarian politics, already tested on domestic issues, which "doesn't crush opposition, but rather climbs into different interest groups and manipulates them from the inside" (Pomerantsev 2014b).[45]

Russian propaganda and disinformation strategies have a long history that dates back to the Soviet era, but the advent of social media has provided its agents with a whole new array of tools to elevate the scope,

---

[42] Organic reach is the audience reached via social media without paying or promoting content. For full definition, see https://www.facebook.com/help/285625061456389?helpref=uf_permalink.

[43] According to the New Knowledge report: "The IRA had a roster of themes, primarily social issues, that they repeatedly emphasized and reinforced across their Facebook, Instagram, and YouTube content." Such themes included: "Black culture, community, Black Lives Matter; Blue Lives Matter, pro-police; Anti-refugee, pro-immigration reform; Texas culture, community, and pride; Southern culture (Confederate history); Separatist movements and secession; Muslim culture, community, and pride; Christian culture, community, and pride; LGBT culture, community, and pride; Native American culture, community, and pride; Meme and 'red pill' culture; Patriotism and Tea Party culture; Liberal and feminist culture; Veteran's Issues; Gun rights, pro-2nd Amendment; Political Pro-Trump, anti-Clinton content; Pro-Bernie Sanders and Jill Stein content; Syria and ISIS, pro-Assad, anti-U.S.; Trust in media".

[44] Weiss, B. (2018). "A Russian troll factory had a $1.25 million monthly budget to interfere in the 2016 US election". *Business Insider.* https://www.businessinsider.com/russian-troll-farm-spent-millions-on-election-interference-2018-2.

[45] Pomerantsev (2014b).

reach and complexity of their efforts. With social media, Russian influence agents have mastered the art of propaganda by manipulating online conversations, spreading false narratives and turning unaware American citizens into puppets of a kind of political theater. The IRA should thus be regarded as an update for the twenty-first century of the Soviet-era 'actives measures,' a series of action of information warfare which included, among other things, media manipulations, disinformation and propaganda campaigns. The most well known of the Russian active measures operation of the past was probably *Operation Infektion*, a disinformation campaign run in the 1980s by KGB agents by planting in small publications worldwide the rumor that the AIDS virus had been developed by US scientists as a part of a biological warfare program.[46]

The Russian strategy was not limited to Facebook, and it involved all the major social media such as Twitter, Instagram, YouTube, Tumblr as well as news aggregator Reddit. Instagram was also leveraged, particularly after Facebook started to become more scrutinized by US officials and law enforcement.[47] In 2017, executives from these technology companies testified in front of the US Senate Select Committee on Intelligence in order to clarify their responsibility in facilitating foreign meddling with American politics. Twitter, for example, disclosed 37,000 Russian accounts whose tweets were seen about 300 million times.[48] YouTube also admitted a heavy presence of Russian trolls, with over a thousand videos distributed on many of its channels. In a belated response to the mounting

---

[46] For an overview of Soviet-era active measures, see Times Video. "Operation Infektion". *The New York Times*. https://www.nytimes.com/video/what-is-disinformation-fake-news-playlist. It is worth pointing out that to this day, 40% of African-Americans believe that AIDS was created by the US government.

[47] As suggested by the already mentioned New Knowledge report, it is also possible that Instagram was chosen also because it lends itself better to the circulation of viral political content in the form of visual memes.

[48] "The indictments revealed one successful example of a Twitter account managed by the IRA under the handle @TEN_GOP, pretending to speak on behalf of the Tennessee Republican Party, which attracted more than 100,000 followers and which was retweeted several times by Donald Trump Jr. The account also actively pushed claims of voter fraud, which would become a mantra for Donald Trump". See Graham, D. (2018). "What Mueller's indictment reveals". *The Atlantic*. https://www.theatlantic.com/politics/archive/2018/02/mueller-roadmap/553604/.

public pressure and official scrutiny on their role as vessels of Russian propaganda, the major American technology companies have acted to remove all the accounts that were associated with the IRA.

2.5 Conclusions

The disinformation and manipulation tactics and strategies against the United States are a clear indication that Russia is deploying an aggressive and ambition foreign policy doctrine vis-à-vis its historical rival. American officials, politicians, journalists and academics are beginning to appreciate the scope and the complexity of the propaganda apparatus that Russian has been developing since 2011–2012, first for domestic purposes and then to exert greater influence in the international arena. Russian propaganda works by combining traditional tight control of the media, censorship and Soviet-era *dezinformacija*, with a more advanced approach to propaganda based on exploiting the free circulation of information via digital technologies.

As seen in the case of the Facebook events staged by the IRA, social media have been weaponized by Russian agents in order to instill doubts and spread controversy. In an ironic twist, the very tools created by American high-tech companies to facilitate business and social exchanges have been used to target American society and politics. Facebook, probably the most sophisticated targeting platform for digital marketers, operates on a business model and algorithmic style of management that incentivizes users' engagement on viral posts. The networking platform has, however, been criticized for amplifying sensational and misleading content that fueled misinformation and partisanship (Benkler et al. 2018; Vaidhyanathan 2018). Russian operatives were quick to discover the potential of Facebook for waging influence operations.

Since Russia is currently not able to compete with America from a military or economic standpoint, it has invested in cultural and technological resources to boost its standing as world power. Russia has indeed rightly understood that the twenty-first century is an information-driven century, and that soft power and hard power are equally important. Under Putin, the Kremlin has put a unique spin on the concept of soft power, stretching it to include propaganda and disinformation campaign as essential elements of its foreign policy strategy (Van Herpen 2016). Just as in the Baltic region and in Ukraine, Russia amplified ethno-political grievances and divisions, in the United States, it exploited race and various cultural or political cleavages. In an age of 'non-linear warfare,' as per Surkov's vision, military attack or occupation of another country is not a requisite for waging warfare, and equally important damage can be achieved with a cyberattack or a vast scale media influence operation.

As seen, Russian strategy was aimed at attacking American societies' fault-lines in order to pit different groups against each other. Socioeconomic divisions linked to structural and cyclic issues with capitalist economy, deeply rooted racial tensions, culture wars on values and lifestyle choices: all of these issues have been plaguing American society for several decades now. Russians decided to expose, amplify and exploit such issues in order to weaken American social and political stability and undermine its democratic process. In carrying their influence campaigns in the United States, Russians have demonstrated cunning cynicism, and no divisive issue has been spared from the repertoire of manipulation, including the highly controversial and potentially dangerous issue of children vaccination. Researchers have in fact detected attempts from Russian trolls and bots to manipulate the on-line conversation on vaccines. As for many other issues, Russian trolls supported both sides, sending pro and anti-vaccine communications to stoke polarization on such a sensitive issue. By playing both sides, again the ultimate goal was to create confusion and erode public consensus and trust in public and government institution responsible for vaccines administration.[49] The organizing of Facebook events by the IRA thus parallels the political practices originally tested for Russian domestic politics, or, as Kakutani (2018, 243) eloquently puts it, "some of the Russian operatives' moves seemed like cynical pieces of Surkovian stagecraft."

The backdrop to these tactics of public opinion division and manipulation is the rampant political polarization that is plaguing American society. As traditional ideological divisions are being supplanted by identity politics, belonging to a political group or movement has become an identity issue even more than an expression of support for a specific policy or program. Political identities have become channels through which one can express personal or affective dimension such as sexual, ethnic, cultural

[49] Glenza, J. (2018). "Russian trolls 'spreading discord' over vaccine safety online". *The Guardian*. https://www.theguardian.com/society/2018/aug/23/russian-trolls-spread-vaccine-misinformation-on-twitter.

or geographic.[50] Political identity differences are thus charged with values drawn from both the public and the private spheres, and this could explain why political cleavages have become so entrenched.

Such emotional and cultural predisposition toward ideological division and infighting makes the American citizens vulnerable to external manipulation efforts, as demonstrated by the case study discussed in this chapter. With respect to this, Foreign Policy magazine comments that "Whether for ideological, tribal, partisan, financial, or other reasons, Americans may simply not be interested in truly understanding and critiquing the information that they receive. Because of that, they will be increasingly the targets of "like wars" by aggressors foreign and domestic."[51]

This fits well with the role of Russia as a raider of globalization that cunningly manipulated technological platforms and information flows to undermine the American democratic process, with the goal of challenging established geopolitical orders. As we shall see in Chapters 3 and 4, such approach does not simply appeal to Russia, but also to other countries that bear resentment against Western powers and against American political supremacy. According to Pomerantsev, the geopolitical conflicts of the twenty-first century are likely to be played out not so much around traditional political categories, such as right vs left, or communism vs capitalism, but between competing visions of globalization, between the somehow naïve Western idea of a 'global village' ruled by liberal democracy and free-market capitalism, which has become increasingly unpopular and untenable, and the emerging Russian notion of 'non-linear war.'[52]

[50] Taub, A. (2017). "Why Americans vote 'against their interest': Partisanship". *The New York Times*. https://www.nytimes.com/2017/04/12/upshot/why-americans-vote-against-their-interest-partisanship.html.

[51] Zenko, M. (2018). "The problem isn't fake news from Russia. It's us". *Foreign Policy*. https://foreignpolicy.com/2018/10/03/the-problem-isnt-fake-news-from-russia-its-us/.

[52] Pomerantsev (2014c).

REFERENCES

Benkler, J. et al. (2018). *Network propaganda: Manipulation, disinformation, and radicalization in American politics.* Oxford, UK: Oxford University Press.

Bennett, W. L., & Livingston, S. (2018). The disinformation order: Disruptive communication and the decline of democratic institutions. *European Journal of Communication, 33*(2), 122–139.

Chen, A. (2015). The agency. An investigation into the Russian troll farm called the Internet Research Agency. *The New York Times Magazine.* https://www.nytimes.com/2015/06/07/magazine/the-agency.html.

Confessore, N., & Wakabayashi, D. (2017). How Russia harvested American rage to reshape US politics. *The New York Times.* https://www.nytimes.com/2017/10/09/technology/russia-election-facebook-ads-rage.html.

Cosentino, G. (2017). *L'era della post-verità. Media e populismi dalla Brexit a Trump.* Reggio Emilia: Imprimatur.

Curtis, A. (2016). Hypernormalization. *BBC.*

D'Ancona, M. (2017). *Post-truth: The new war on truth and how to fight back.* London: Ebury Press.

DiResta, D., et al. (2018). *The tactics & tropes of the internet research agency* (p. 6). New Knowledge.

Dixon, J. (2016). Is Vladislav Surkov an artist? *New Minds Eye.* https://newmindseye.wordpress.com/is-vladislav-surkov-an-artist/.

Engström, M. (2014). Contemporary Russian messianism and new Russian foreign policy. *Contemporary Security Policy, 35*(2), 356–379. https://doi.org/10.1080/13523260.2014.965888.

Harsin, J. (2018). Post-truth and critical communication. *Oxford Research Encyclopedias.* https://doi.org/10.1093/acrefore/9780190228613.013.757.

Kakutani, M. (2018). *The death of truth.* New York: Tim Duggan Books.

Milam, W. (2018). Who is Vladislav Surkov? *Medium.* https://medium.com/@wmilam/the-theater-director-who-is-vladislav-surkov-9dd8a15e0efb.

Pariser, E. (2011). *The filter bubble. How the New Personalized Web Is Changing What We Read and How We Think.* New York: Penguin.

Pomerantsev, P. (2011). Putin's Rasputin. *London Review of Books.* https://www.lrb.co.uk/v33/n20/peter-pomerantsev/putins-rasputin.

Pomerantsev, P. (2014a). The hidden author of Putinism. How Vladislav Surkov invented the new Russia. *The Atlantic.* https://www.theatlantic.com/international/archive/2014/11/hidden-author-putinism-russia-vladislav-surkov/382489/.

Pomerantsev, P. (2014b). Russia's ideology: There is no truth. *The New York Times.* https://www.nytimes.com/2014/12/12/opinion/russias-ideology-there-is-no-truth.html.

Pomerantsev, P., & Weiss, M. (2014). The menace of unreality: How the Kremlin weaponizes information, culture and money. *The Interpreter.*

Roudakova, N. (2017). *Losing Pravda: Ethics and the press in post-truth Russia*. Cambridge: Cambridge University Press.

Seddon, M. (2014). Documents show how Russia's troll army hit America. *Buzzfeed*. https://www.buzzfeednews.com/article/maxseddon/documents-show-how-russias-troll-army-hit-america.

Snyder, T. (2018). *The road to unfreedom: Russia, Europe, America*. New York: Tim Duggan Books.

Tucker, J., et al. (2018). Social media, political polarization, and political disinformation: A review of the scientific literature. *SSRN Electronic Journal*. https://doi.org/10.2139/ssrn.3144139.

Vaidhyanathan, S. (2018). *Anti-social media. How Facebook disconnects us and undermines democracy*. Oxford: Oxford University Press.

Van Herpen, M. (2016). *Putin's propaganda machine soft power and Russian foreign policy*. Maryland: Rowman & Littlefield.

Woolley, S., & Howard, P. (2018). *Computational propaganda*. Oxford, UK: Oxford University Press.

CHAPTER 3

From Pizzagate to the Great Replacement: The Globalization of Conspiracy Theories

Abstract This chapter discusses the circulation of conspiracy theories evolving from concoctions of Internet subcultures to global topics of public conversation and political mobilization. The examples provided are those of the Pizzagate and QAnon conspiracy theories, which embody the anti-establishment ethos, the paranoid disposition and the ironic attitude of far-right on-line communities. The chapter analyzes the spreading of a set of myths, symbols and codes created by the 4chan and 8chan users within a global network of White ethnonationalists. The far-right anti-immigration conspiracy theory 'The Great Replacement' is discussed to explore the interlocking themes of White identity politics, trolling and the 'weaponization' of Internet entertainment.

Keywords Conspiracy theories · Pizzagate · QAnon · Great Replacement · Meme · Ethnonationalism · Alt-right

3.1 Introduction

This chapter discusses the global circulation of conspiracy theories, with a special emphasis on fictional political narratives originating from Internet message boards and discussion forums. Specifically, the focus of the analysis is on conspiracy theories alleging plots by global liberal elites or progressive movements, popular among White supremacists and far-right

G. Cosentino, *Social Media and the Post-Truth World Order*,
https://doi.org/10.1007/978-3-030-43005-4_3

circles. The chapter attempts to trace a profile of the most popular conspiracy theories currently dominating the discourse among users of fringe spaces of the Internet, especially 4chan, 8chan and Reddit. Such on-line conversations, often cloaked in ironic language, emerge from a subcultural milieu that has been conducive to acts of on-line harassment as well as of violence and terrorism. The 2016 Pizzagate conspiracy theory is presented as the blueprint for fictional political narratives growing out of the contributions of multiple authors in various world regions. The QAnon conspiracy theory, an offshoot of Pizzagate, is also presented as an open-ended collective narrative based on paranoid attitudes toward political institutions and establishments, typical of the current era of Internet-driven populism and radical politics. The chapter also discusses how the conspiracy theories under examination functioned as outlets for the collective elaboration of unaddressed political scandals.

In the second part of the chapter, the 'Great Replacement' conspiracy theory is discussed as a narrative of victimization of people of White ethnicity, serving as an ideological framework for a growing wave of violent actions by White nationalists worldwide. The on-line communications of White terrorists are brought under examination as they crystallize many aesthetic, cultural and ideological elements common to other on-line subcultures and movements mobilizing around claims of marginalization and dispossession. Memes and other elements of Internet popular culture are discussed as ideologically charged resources of on-line culture wars. Reference to post-truth theory is offered throughout the chapter to place the discussion of on-line conspiracy theories within the broader conceptual framework presented in the book's introduction.

3.2   Pizzagate: The Blueprint for Global On-Line Conspiracy Theories

One of the most absurd and creative of the many fictional political narratives circulating in the 2016 US presidential election cycle—characterized by large amounts of misinformation and disinformation, especially via social media[1]—was the conspiracy theory[2] that went by the name of 'Pizzagate.' The theory alleged that Comet Ping Pong, a Washington pizzeria, was the operational base of a high-profile ring of pedophiles and Satanists, which included top political figures of the Democratic Party such as the then presidential candidate Hillary Clinton and her former campaign manager John Podesta. Even before a self-styled vigilante named Edgar Welch decided to approach this odd story armed with weapons,[3] an investigation by the Washington Police Department had already dismissed Pizzagate as a baseless conspiracy theory, mostly circulating on-line via discussion forums, anonymous imageboards, right-wing alternative news sources and social media accounts (Marwick and Lewis 2017). Articles from The New York Times[4] and Snopes[5] reported that there was no evidence in support of the allegations against Comet Ping Pong. These revelations had, however, not prevented many to continue to believe in the existence of a sordid scandal. On the contrary, the debunking, as it is often the case in context of post-truth concoctions such as conspiracy theories, had the effect of further stoking the suspicions among the Pizzagate proponents. For the entire month of November 2016, after the story had been repeatedly dismissed by mainstream

[1] Allcott, H., & Gentzkow, M. (2017). "Social media and fake news in the 2016 election". *Journal of Economic Perspectives* 31:2, 211–236. See also Singer and Booking (2018).

[2] In his work *A culture of conspiracy*, Barkun defines a conspiracy theory as being based on "the belief that an organization made up of individuals or groups was or is acting covertly to achieve some malevolent end" (Barkun 2013, 3).

[3] On a Sunday in early December 2016, less than a month after the election of Donald Trump as the 45th President of the United States, a man named Edgar Welch entered Comet Ping Pong brandishing an AR-15 assault rifle. He then asked all the clients to evacuate the place and started searching the premises looking for a basement connected to secret underground tunnels. The police arrived shortly after Welch had fired a few shots on the floor, with no injuries or casualties. By his own admission, he wanted to 'self-investigate' Comet Ping Pong, to see if the on-line rumors about the so-called *Pizzagate* conspiracy theory were true. He had read a lot about Pizzagate, including accounts from notorious conspiracy-theorist Alex Jones, and had come to Washington with the intention of freeing the children who he thought were kept enslaved in the basement of the pizzeria.

[4] Kang, C. (2016). "Fake news onslaught targets pizzeria as nest of child-trafficking". *The New York Times*. https://www.nytimes.com/2016/11/21/technology/fact-check-this-pizzeria-is-not-a-child-trafficking-site.html.

[5] Lacapria, K. (2016). "Is Comet Ping Pong Pizzeria home to a child abuse ring led by Hillary Clinton?". *Snopes*. https://www.snopes.com/fact-check/pizzagate-conspiracy/.

media, rumors and speculations around Comet Ping Pong continued to circulate on social media, generating over a million Twitter messages with the hashtag #pizzagate.[6]

According to Craig Silverman of Buzzfeed, one of the first journalists to investigate the association between social media and disinformation, Pizzagate "shows how Trump supporters, members of 4chan and Reddit, and right-wing blogs in the United States and in other countries combined to create and spread viral misinformation during the election season."[7] It also demonstrates how thin are the boundaries between virtual and real repercussions of disinformation, and how "real-world harassment and violence can emerge as a direct result of media manipulation and misinformation online" (Marwick and Lewis 2017, 56). The conspiracy theory is thus a case in point of the multilayered, collaborative and troublesome post-truth dynamics at work during the 2016 US elections, as a plurality of actors motivated by different but overlapping reasons was involved in its creation, circulation and real-life escalation.

The most active sources of allegations behind Pizzagate were the imageboard 4chan and the discussion forum Reddit,[8] popular especially among a variety of Internet subcultures, as well as with people affiliated with the American ethnonationalist far-right, the so-called alt-right.[9] Social media were also instrumental in igniting the conspiracy theory: the first allegation that Hillary Clinton was involved in a pedophile ring was made by a Twitter account associated with White supremacists on October 30, 2016. In a cross-pollination between far-right and anti-Clinton social media users, the tweet referenced a Facebook message by an American woman claiming to have revelations from the New York Police Department about material on the laptop of Anthony Weiner—former US Congressman involved in a 'sexting' scandal with a minor—which suggested that Hillary Clinton was part of a child trafficking ring

---

[6] BBC. (2016). "The Saga of 'Pizzagate': The fake story that shows how conspiracy theories spread". *BBC News*. http://www.bbc.com/news/blogstrending-38156985.

[7] Silverman, C. (2016). "How the bizarre conspiracy theory behind 'Pizzagate' was spread". *Buzzfeed News*. https://www.buzzfeed.com/craigsilverman/fever-swamp-election.

[8] Reddit is an on-line aggregator of news, reviews and discussions, popular especially among hackers and software developers.

[9] Alt-right personalities such as Mike Cernovich were actively involved in promoting Pizzagate.

in association with convicted sex offender Jeffrey Epstein.[10] Revelations about the emails found on Weiner laptop that were relevant to the Hillary Clinton email controversy—possibly the most prominent theme of the 2016 campaign—started to circulate on 4chan and Reddit, stoking fantastic conjectures among their users. Some of these were picked up by both junk-news web sites and 'clickbait fabricators' (Benkler et al. 2018), often styled to appear as legitimate news sources, which were important drivers of disinformation in 2016.

At the same time, many 4chan and Reddit users were sifting through the thousands of emails that been hacked from the mail servers of John Podesta by means of a phishing scam. The hacking, done by two groups of Russian hackers called Fancy Bear and Cozy Bear,[11] had resulted in a leaking by the counter-information site WikiLeaks of a trove of personal email communication of Podesta. When WikiLeaks started making the email available on-line, users of 4chan, in particular those active in the /pol/ discussion group, a virtual meeting place for Trump supporters, searched through them for any information that could be used to damage Hillary Clinton. Some Reddit users, active on the discussion group r/The Donald, also popular among Trump supporters, suggested that the emails contained coded messages alluding to pedophiliac practices. The term 'pizza,' for example, frequently recurring in the email exchanges of Podesta, was alleged to be used by the pedophile ring to suggest 'underage girls.'[12] This is when the various rumors started to be collected in a common narrative that was labeled Pizzagate. After such narrative involving Comet Ping Pong appeared on 4chan and Reddit, Facebook right-wing partisan pages and professional conspiracy theorists like the British David Icke and the American Alex Jones gave wider amplification to the initial rumors and creative elaborations. While a lot of grassroots input

[10] It should be noted that conspiracy theories on the alleged links between the Clintons and pedophiliac rings have also been popular among right-wing circles for years, especially since revelations were made public in the mid-2000s on the friendship between Bill Clinton and Jeffrey Epstein, a wealthy hedge-fund manager and convicted sex offender.

[11] "One was allegedly associated with the GRU, Russian military intelligence, the other was possibly associated with the FSB (successor to the KGB)" (Benkler et al. 2018, 239).

[12] James Alefantis, the owner of Comet Ping Pong, was involved in the conspiracy theory because his name had appeared in the email exchanges with Podesta, when the two were discussing the possibility of organizing a fundraising at the pizzeria.

went into popularizing Pizzagate, the role of Alex Jones and of other social media conspirations was crucial. Pizzagate thus shows "how online virality—far from a measure of sincere popularity—is a force that can be manipulated and sustained by just a few influential social media accounts" (Singer and Brooking 2018, 404). This observation is also valid for the role of social media influencers amplifying Russian propaganda in the context of the Syrian Civil War, as discussed in the next chapter.

The Pizzagate conspiracy theory took shape as a collective mythology by means of a collaborative storytelling via social media, imageboards, discussion forums and other alternative on-line information outlets, which was amplified by post-truth influencers and entrepreneurs. A fantastic narrative that nonetheless had all the characteristics to excite and mobilize the most radical fringes among Donald Trump supporters and even some people close to the Trump administration (Neiwert 2017). What makes this conspiracy theory particularly interesting is of course its timing, right before the 2016 US presidential elections, as its exposure and resonance were magnified by an electoral cycle characterized by a highly polarized and aggressive public discourse, which has proved fertile ground for the circulation of misinformation and disinformation (Benkler et al. 2018).

Pizzagate had also clear connections with another problematic aspect of the 2016 election cycle, namely the Russian cyberattacks and media manipulation strategies to influence the American democratic process, as discussed in the previous chapter. The hacking of the Podesta emails made possible by the actions of Russian hackers, allegedly under direct supervision of the Kremlin,[13] was in fact the initial spark of the Pizzagate conspiracy theory. Also, means of computational propaganda (Woolley and Howard 2018) linked to Russian manipulation and influence tactics played a role on the amplification of Pizzagate, as "a combination of bots and bot-like accounts were used to make the topic trend, suggest grass-roots activity, and provide enough legitimacy that real people were inspired to join in" (Marwick and Lewis 2017, 38).

---

[13] Russian hackers, according to preliminary investigation by US authorities, were operating under the direct supervision of Vladimir Putin, even though the Kremlin denied any allegations, admitting only the possibility that some Russian hackers had been overly 'patriotic'. See McIntire, M. (2016). "How a Putin fan overseas pushed pro-Trump propaganda to Americans". *The New York Times*. https://www.nytimes.com/2016/12/17/world/europe/russia-propaganda-elections.html.

The sudden popularization of Pizzagate is an indication of the unique dynamics that were at work during the 2016 American elections. All the actors involved in the 'epistemic crisis' (Benkler et al. 2018) plaguing that election cycle operated jointly: foreign actors, associated with antagonistic governments,[14] engaged in operations of media manipulation in the form of leaking of sensitive information, which resulted in the circulation of disinformation via on-line networked communities of trolls, far-right activists, social media, alternative news outlets, fake news factories and political influencers. Such vast seeding of disinformation, amplified by social media algorithms favoring sensational content, found a receptive ground in the ideological milieu of far-right or populist movements, as in the case of the American ethnonationalist far-right, which welcomed any type of information or narratives that could be used to mobilize their base against establishment politicians, and to challenge the discourse of the so-called mainstream liberal media.[15]

Given the global nature of Pizzagate, which is a case in point for the complexity of the current flows of on-line disinformation, it should not be surprising to find out that the conspiracy theory resonated well beyond the American borders. The so-called junk news and clickbait entrepreneurs active out of Veles,[16] Macedonia, a major producer of disinformation on the 2016 election cycle, feasted on Pizzagate and participated to the further elaboration and circulation on the original allegations about Comet Ping Pong, adding new fictional elements to its core narrative.

Pizzagate was also for a while also a sensitive political topic in Turkey, where in late 2016 a group of supporters of Turkish President Erdogan started to spread the same rumors on Comet Ping Pong that had been circulating in the United States. Social media accounts and trolls affiliated with the Erdogan AK party (Bulut and Yörük 2017) were at the forefront of the disinformation effort, supported by the main national media, which

---

[14] Calabresi, M., & Rebala, P. (2016). "Here's the evidence Russia hacked the democratic national committee". *Time Magazine*. http://time.com/4600177/election-hack-russia-hillary-clinton-donald-trump.

[15] Confessore, N., & Wakabayashi, D. (2017). "How Russia harvested American rage to reshape U.S. politics". *The New York Times*. https://www.nytimes.com/2017/10/09/technology/russia-election-facebook-ads-rage.html.

[16] Subramanian, S. (2017). "The Macedonian Teens who mastered fake news". *Wired*. https://www.wired.com/2017/02/veles-macedonia-fake-news.

popularized the alleged scandal to the broader Turkish public.[17] The pro-Erdogan Turkish commentators expediently took the Pizzagate scandal as an indication of the moral corruption of Western leaders, above all Hillary Clinton, thus tapping on the similar rhetoric against liberal and globalist leaders used by populist and nationalist politicians such as Donald Trump in United States or Nigel Farage and Boris Johnson in the UK. Writing on the subject on *The Daily Dot*, Turkish journalist and researcher Efrem Sozeri argued that Pizzagate was a case of a truly far-right global conspiracy theory, appealing to both White nationalists in the United States and right-wing Islamist nationalists in Turkey. In a whirlwind of misinformation and disinformation on a global scale, a Twitter account named @pizza_gate, which for a while was one of the main sources of updates on the alleged scandal, turned out to be equally popular among conspiracy theorists in the United States as in Turkey.

The Turkish interest for Pizzagate, and its reverberations on Western media, illustrates very well how post-truth as a global condition currently occurs within complex networks of reiterations, modifications and amplifications of false information extending beyond national borders. Such fictional narratives can become political expedients in contexts that are completely different from those in which they were born. At the same time, the global feedback on the Pizzagate reinforced the belief among American conspiracy theorists and right-wing voters, and the involvement of Turkish media was as unexpected as it was timely for the supporters of Donald Trump.

One of the most significant aspects of the Pizzagate incident was the already mentioned inability of the verification process by official authorities and mainstream media to change the belief of the conspiracy theory proponents. Fact-checking efforts ended up backfiring and stoking even further the suspicions among believers. This fits Harsin's theory that in the post-truth condition, debunking and verification are rarely effective

---

[17] The Turkish pro-government media became interested in Pizzagate as a form of retaliation against domestic critics and opponents of the president, who were accused of not giving the alleged scandal enough attention after they had promoted a very critical campaign against a foundation linked to Erdogan that had been involved in a documented case of pedophilia. See Sozeri, E. (2016). "How the alt-right's PizzaGate conspiracy hid real scandal in Turkey". *The Daily Dot*. https://www.dailydot.com/layer8/pizzagate-alt-right-turkey-trolls-child-abuse/.

since there is no trusted public venue in which authority can definitively debunk disinformation and thus suture the conflicting segments of the public opinion (Harsin 2015).

3.3   From Epstein to QAnon: The Emancipatory and Playful Side of Conspiracy Theories

There is, however, another aspect about the genesis and circulation of Pizzagate that is worth taking into consideration. Uscinski (2017) offers an original reading of conspiracy theories that isn't necessarily concerned with their epistemic value. Instead, he considers conspiracy theories as being eminently 'notions about power' that serve as resources and tools of dissent by the weak and disenfranchised segments of society to off-set against inequality and injustice. Seen through this emancipatory perspective, conspiracy theories offer an outlet of imaginary and imaginative articulation for popular fantasies and aspirations about power, and about challenges to the existing power structure.

In this sense, one could read conspiracy theories as attempts to address the hidden and more opaque aspects of power. Such narrative forms of mobilization against power, while often relying on scarce evidence, on a surplus of fictional elaboration, and only a small kernel of truth, nonetheless play an important role in freeing people's aspirations of political change. As argued by Kalpokas, "menacing narratives that involve (…) plots by malicious others can have a strong 'feel good' factor" and are "efficient in arousing and mobilizing audiences" (Kalpokas 2018, 19). Pizzagate served this function as it presented the elementary narrative structure of the classic conspiracy theory format, based on "archetypal malevolent elites carrying out their dirty deeds behind everybody's back with impunity" (Kalpokas 2018, 19).

Conspiracy theories can thus function as fictions charged with affective and aspirational values, providing the publics with possibility of agency in the construction of emancipatory expressions. Fictional narratives with a paranoid streak such as conspiracy theories operate as forms of co-operation between grassroots aspirational efforts and top-down strategies of public opinion manipulation. While enabled and exploited by foreign agents and also by political influencers such as Alex Jones, Pizzagate also served as an outlet for regular people to express their grievances against the perceived impunity of political and financial elites. This latter function of the conspiracy theory is best encapsulated by the recent revelations surrounding the arrest and subsequent death of disgraced financier and convicted sex offender Jeffrey Epstein, whose name was associated with the Clintons in the original rumors about the child trafficking ring allegedly operating in Washington.

As already discussed, the debunking of Pizzagate, while ineffective in diffusing the anxieties around the fictitious scandal, it nonetheless widely demonstrated that the allegations on Comet Ping Pong were baseless. Even a radical conspiracy theorist such as Alex Jones retracted his initial support for Pizzagate after the incident at the Washington pizzeria.[18] However, months after the violent exploit of Edgar Welch, some supporters of Pizzagate were still convinced that the theory contained some truth, and "expressed frustration that the mainstream news was not taking their concerns seriously and covered the story only dismissively" (Marwick and Lewis 2017), claiming that it deserved a more thorough investigation. This insistence could be explained by acknowledging that there was, in fact, a small element of truth in Pizzagate that did have an actual reference to real events.

The collective storytelling that gave rise to Pizzagate was initially started by a rumor that in fact addressed an element of the judicial case involving Jeffrey Epstein, specifically the reference to the so-called Lolita Express plane that belonged to the millionaire, which he used to bus his elite circle of friends and underage girls to his private islands in the Caribbean.[19] The Epstein case, dating back to 2005, had for many years lingered in the background of the broader political discourse as an example of how powerful people could use their connections to defy justice. In 2008, Jeffrey Epstein was charged by the Palm Beach Police Department for soliciting prostitution with minors. Since 2005, he had also been under investigation by the FBI on the allegation that he had been running a vast trafficking and cult-like sex enslavement ring involving dozens of

[18] Fahri, P. (2017). "Conspiracy theorist Alex Jones backs off 'Pizzagate' claims". *The Washington Post*. https://www.washingtonpost.com/lifestyle/style/conspiracy-theorist-alex-jones-backs-off-pizzagate-claims/2017/03/24/6f0246fe-10cd-11e7-ab07-07d9f521f6b5_story.html.

[19] Bryan, N. (2015). "Flight logs put Clinton, Dershowitz on Pedophile Billionaire's sex jet". *Gawker*. https://gawker.com/flight-logs-put-clinton-dershowitz-on-pedophile-billio-1681039971.

underage girls across multiple locations. However, Epstein was only sentenced for his lesser crimes, and the FBI investigation on the more serious crimes was blocked when Epstein entered into discussions for a plea deal with then Miami US Attorney Alexander Acosta.[20] The deal signed by Epstein was kept secret, and the sentence he received is considered to be the most lenient ever received by a serious sex offender.[21]

In July 2019, the FBI arrested Epstein with new charges of sex trafficking with minors and conspiracy to engage in sex trafficking minors, and the following month, he was found dead in his cell in a Manhattan correctional facility. The circumstances surrounding Epstein death became immediately fertile ground for further conspiracy theories, which echoed some of the elements of the original Pizzagate narrative, suggesting the existence of a powerful cabal of political and financial elites who feared his possible confessions after his arrest.[22] In the aftermath of his death, Donald Trump retweeted a message by a right-wing personality alleging that the Clintons were involved in the murder of Epstein. In the now global amplification process of conspiracy theories, Russian information channels such as RT and Sputnik dedicated coverage to Epstein's suspicious death in jail. Two rival hashtags, #clintonbodycountand #trumpbodycount, went viral at the time, pushing opposing theories about the involvement with his death in prison of either the Clintons or Trump, who both had been associated with Epstein in the past.[23]

As one commentator observed, "the circumstances of Epstein's life and career are essentially tailor-made to produce conspiracy theories (…)

[20] Ward, V. (2019). "Jeffrey Epstein's sick story played out for years in plain sight". *The Daily Beast.* https://www.thedailybeast.com/jeffrey-epsteins-sick-story-played-out-for-years-in-plain-sight?ref=scroll.

[21] Epstein served only 13 months in a county jail with extensive work release and privileged treatment, when he could have faced up to 45 years in a federal prison. See Brown, J., & Albright, A. (2018). "Perversion of justice". *Miami Herald.* https://www.miamiherald.com/news/local/article221897990.html.

[22] Epstein's cellmate was removed without replacement, the security guards fell asleep while on watch and the camera in front of his cells was malfunctioning. See Benner, K., & Ivory, D. (2019). "Jeffrey Epstein death: 2 guards slept through checks and falsified records". *The New York Times.* https://www.nytimes.com/2019/08/13/nyregion/jeffrey-epstein-jail-officers.html.

[23] Beggin, R. (2019). "Trump again boosts a baseless conspiracy theory, this one about Jeffrey Epstein". *Vox.* https://www.vox.com/policy-and-politics/2019/8/11/20800787/jeffrey-epstein-donald-trump-conspiracy-theory-clinton-body-count-retweet-killed-death-by-suicide.

because so many of the most important questions about how Epstein gained and retained his power have gone unanswered."[24] Some speculations suggested that Epstein's main business was "collecting footage or other evidence of his powerful friends having sex with underage girls so he could force the men to invest money with him."[25] Other rumors pointed to his involvement with the US government. During his testimony to the Trump transition team, Acosta said that at the time of the plea deal he was told that "Epstein 'belonged to intelligence' and to leave it alone."[26] Both allegations fit of course well with the basic conspiracy theory frame of powerful groups scheming secretly, with the assistance of State apparatuses, to advance illicit agendas. The fact that they have been lingering as unaddressed or even suppressed issues for many years reinforces the collective suspicions about the political establishment that allowed Epstein to defy justice.

Pizzagate thus operated as a form of collective and spontaneous elaboration, based on a kernel of truth, of the largely unaddressed Epstein scandal, which one Epstein victims called a "conspiracy that a lot of powerful people wanted to go away."[27] The core narrative element of Pizzagate—the existence of a child trafficking ring among powerful elites—represented a sort of repressed or hidden truth that was channeled through a storytelling in the form of a conspiracy theory. In this sense, one is tempted to agree with Uscinski bold claim that "conspiracy theories are necessary to the healthy functioning of a society because they help balance against concentrations of power" (Uscisnki 2017, 2). This reading of the phenomenon echoes the interpretation of post-truth communications as 'aspirational emancipatory counternarratives,' which can offer an immediately gratifying, albeit elusive, forms of political action for the 'marginalized and the alienated,' as argued by Kalpokas.

With some many unanswered questions surrounding the life and death of Epstein, it shouldn't surprise that the core of suspicion at the heart of

[24] North, A. (2019). "Why the Jeffrey Epstein case inspires so many conspiracy theories". *Vox.* https://www.vox.com/identities/2019/8/14/20803950/jeffrey-epstein-conspiracy-theories-clinton-trump-acosta.

[25] Ibid.

[26] Ibid.

[27] 60 Minutes Australia. "Exposing Jeffrey Epstein's international sex trafficking ring". https://www.youtube.com/watch?v=VQOOxOl9l80.

Pizzagate survived even after the fading of the conspiracy theory. Pizzagate in a sense didn't die out, but it simply morphed into a different, even more complex conspiracy theory going by the name of QAnon. QAnon emerged in October 2017, again by means of its circulation via 4chan, sharing the same narrative core as Pizzagate: the existence of a secret global child sex ring run by liberal political and financial elites. Unlike Pizzagate, QAnon posited also the involvement of so-called deep state entities.[28] But just as with Pizzagate, QAnon storytelling hints to the core elements of the Epstein scandal that remain undisclosed and unaddressed, especially the role of well-connected politicians, businessman and celebrities involved in the child trafficking ring. With a further fictional twist on the basic Pizzagate storytelling, QAnon proponents also claim that the Mueller investigation on Trump's alleged collusion with Russia was in fact just a cover-up for what was instead a secret collaboration between the two to bring down the alleged global child sex ring.[29]

The name QAnon is a reference to the highest security clearance available in the Department of Energy in the US government, allowing access to information about nuclear weapons. A 4Chan user called Q Clearance Patriot, or simply Q, claiming to have top security clearance, started to post with relative frequency cryptic messages—'bread crumbs' or QDrops in the parlance of its followers—often written as riddles, aimed at sparking people curiosity on a series of political issues. The posts then became material for speculation and investigation by the broader community of 4chan, who collectively elaborated on Q's posts. The conspiracy theory thus evolved as a collection of various political concoctions, also going under the title of 'The Storm' or 'The Great Awakening,' revolving around a common theme, that is the role of Donald Trump as savior of regular American citizens against the scheming of political elites and State

---

[28] The 'deep state' is a conspiracy theory suggesting the clandestine existence of a shadow or hidden power system of governmental and non-governmental entities, relying on cronyism and collusion, within the legitimately elected government.

[29] Because of its delirious and convoluted narrative, some have even speculated that QAnon is in fact the product of an elaborate hoax against Trump supporters, inspired by the work of Italian activist collective Luther Blissett. According to this interpretation, QAnon was meant at poking fun at right-wing conspiracy theories and their supporters, but it was taken seriously by imageboards members and it eventually spiraled out of control. See Davis, B. (2018). "Is the QAnon conspiracy the work of artist-activist pranksters? The evidence for (and against) a dangerous hypothesis". *Artnet*. https://news.artnet.com/opinion/q-anon-hoax-1329983.

apparatuses. As a result, QAnons have become closely associated with the broader community of Trump supporters, and QAnon t-shirts and signs frequently appear at Trump events.

Another element of similarity between the Pizzagate and QAnon is their nature of collaborative and playful storytelling emerging out of the subcultural milieu of imageboards. The various plot twists of the QAnon narrative, ranging from the implausible to the ludicrous, often just ended up adding ironic layers to the basic set of beliefs, legitimate as it might be for some proponents of the theory. Irony and provocation are integral to the conversations occurring on imageboards, and fictional elaborations are often exaggerated in order to trigger reactions in the media or among the broader public opinion (Nagle 2017; Phillips 2015). QAnon pushed the collaborative and playful angle even further by making the participation in the conspiracy theory as a kind of role-playing game. As commented by Alyssa Rosenberg in the Washington Post, QAnon added an element of so-called gamification, or the application of game principles, to the standard process of elaboration and circulation of conspiracy theories: "The best way to think of QAnon may be not as a conspiracy theory, but as an unusually absorbing alternate-reality game with extremely low barriers to entry. The 'Q' poster's cryptic missives give believers a task to complete on a semiregular basis. Even more so than conventional video games (…) QAnon is open-ended."[30] The game-like participation in QAnon is one of its most appealing aspects, and it reflects a common trait of on-line conspiracy theory and on-line harassment campaigns, which entice new members with entertaining experience such as scoring points, gaining status within the community or increasing its visibility. This is of course also a reflection of the subcultural milieu of 4chan, infused with reference to videogame culture (Phillips 2015).

As with Pizzagate, also QAnon migrated from on-line to real life, thanks to its popularization via an extensive media coverage, support by celebrities and its game-like nature. However, just like with its precursor, the transition to real life didn't occur without violent repercussions. In May 2019, after a series of violent crimes associated with QAnon believers, including the murder of a mafia boss, the FBI identified QAnon as a domestic terrorist threat, making it the first fringe conspiracy theory to be

---

[30] Rosenberg, A. (2019). "I understand the temptation to dismiss QAnon. Here's why we can't". *Washington Post*. https://www.washingtonpost.com/opinions/2019/08/07/qanon-isnt-just-conspiracy-theory-its-highly-effective-game/.

labeled as such. An FBI memo on the subject said that "conspiracy theories very likely will emerge, spread, and evolve in the modern information marketplace, occasionally driving both groups and individual extremists to carry out criminal or violent acts."[31]

While one can acknowledge, like Uscinski and Kalpokas do, that conspiracy theories can perform a politically and emotionally liberating function for their supporters—as it was revealed by the Epstein case—there remains a fundamentally problematic aspect about the construction of simplistic and paranoid political narratives intent at obfuscating evidence-based investigations and official accounts. As commented by a researcher on QAnon, such a complex and multilayered conspiracy theory can function and spread since society now operates as a 'marketplace of realities,'[32] a notion that echoes Harsin's concept of truth-markets (Harsin 2015) as the founding elements of the post-truth condition. Through fantastical collective storytelling and game-like experiences on various contentious political issues, on-line communities have given people the ability to break down a consensual, evidence-based reality and to transform it by bending it to their desires, aspirations or fears, even the most radical or delirious.

3.4   'Remove Kebab': Ethnonationalism Between Memes and Terrorism

In the Facebook Live feed streamed by Brenton Tarrant, the Australian far-right terrorist and White supremacist who killed 51 people in two separate attacks in Christchurch, New Zealand, on March 15, 2019, one particular song, among others, could be heard playing in the attacker's car moments before he began shooting inside the Al Noor mosque. The song is called 'Remove Kebab,' also known as 'Serbia strong,' an Islamophobic and Serbian nationalist song of the turbo-folk genre. The lyrics celebrate Radovan Karadžić, the Bosnian Serb leader in the 1990s Yugoslav wars who was found guilty of genocide against Bosnian Muslims. Since the mid-2000s, the song has gained Internet popularity among a loose

[31] Budryk, Z. (2019). "FBI memo warns QAnon poses potential terror threat: Report". *The Hill*. https://thehill.com/policy/national-security/fbi/455770-fbi-memo-warns-qanon-poses-a-potential-terror-threat-report.

[32] Rosenberg (2019).

community of videogame players and White nationalists.[33] For White supremacists and ethnonationalists active on 4chan and 8chan, the phrase *Remove Kebab* has become a synonym for their Islamophobic inclinations, the most radical of which is the ethnic cleansing of Muslims from Western countries.[34] In the 74-page long document—a manifesto of some sorts entitled 'The Great Replacement'—that Tarrant circulated via Twitter and on 8chan before the attack, he referred to himself as someone who has been "working part time as a Kebab removalist," an ironic presentation of his own anti-Muslim stance as well as an obvious homage to the Internet memes spawned around the 'Remove Kebab' song.

The title of Tarrant's manifesto, where he laid out the background and the motivations behind his murderous actions, cloaking them in a humorous language full of subcultural references, hints to the Great Replacement conspiracy theory, a recurring theme in the rhetoric of far-right nationalist movements. While circulating among European right-wing circles for over a century, the conspiracy theory was recently re-popularized by French author Renaud Camus, who claims that technocratic elites in France and in Europe are responsible for a plan aimed at replacing Europeans of White ethnicity with immigrants of different ethnicity, particularly from Muslim countries.

In his 2011 work *Le Grand Remplacement*, Camus blames industrialization and capitalism for encouraging mass immigration, unregulated demographic growth among immigrants and low birth rate among White Westerners. These factors are considered to be parts of the engineered substitution of the White European ethnicity and cultural tradition by Muslim immigrants, actively pursued by a loosely defined transnational

---

[33] Novislav Dajić, the song's accordion player, himself convicted for multiple murders during the war, has become a widespread 4chan meme as "Dat Face Soldier". See https://en.wikipedia.org/wiki/Remove_Kebab.

[34] "A YouTube video for the song (…) shows emaciated Muslim prisoners in Serb-run detention camps during the war. 'Beware Ustashas and Turks' says the song, using wartime, derogatory terms for Bosnian Croats and Bosnian Muslims used by Serb nationalists." See Gec, J. (2019). "Suspected New Zealand gunman fascinated with Ottoman wars, named rifles after legendary Serbs". *The Morning Call*. https://www.mcall.com/news/breaking/mc-nws-new-zealand-shooter-balkans-20190316-story.html.

elite that Camus calls the 'Davos-cracy'[35]—from the Davos summit—
consisting of liberal politicians and business executives for whom workers are replaceable elements without any connection to their homeland or
cultural heritage. "We are experiencing an invasion on a level never seen
before in history. Millions of people pouring across our borders, legally.
Invited by the state and corporate entities to replace the White people"
write Tarrant in his manifesto.[36]

The Great Replacement theory parallels that of the 'White Genocide,'
another trope of contemporary White nationalist and supremacist discourse and propaganda (Neiwert 2017). It refers to the idea that the
genetic and cultural heritage of White people in the United States is
being jeopardized or even annihilated by means of miscegenation and
forced assimilation with non-White immigrants. The conspiracy theory
was made popular by American neo-Nazi David Lane in his 1995 *White
Genocide Manifesto*, where he placed explicit blame on Jewish elites for
allegedly masterminding the plot. While the Great Replacement is at its
core an Islamophobic belief, Lane's ideology is anti-Semitic. The parallel themes of the Great Replacement and of White Genocide have both
antecedents in right-wing politics during the decolonization era in Europe
and in post-Civil War America,[37] and in recent years, they have become
central tenets of a global discourse of White supremacists and far-right
terrorists responsible for violent acts in multiple countries, as well of the
rhetoric of right-wing political parties and populist movements both in
Europe[38] and in the United States (Davey and Ebner 2019). Brenton
Tarrant made reference to both conspiracy theories in his manifesto, and

[35] Wilson, A. (2019). "Fear-filled apocalypses: The far-right's use of conspiracy theories". *Oxford Research Group*. https://www.oxfordresearchgroup.org.uk/blog/fear-filled-
apocalypses-the-far-rights-use-of-conspiracy-theory.

[36] Tarrant, B. (2019). *The great replacement* (p. 2). http://tarrantmanifesto.com/.

[37] Schwartzburg, R. (2019). "No, there isn't a White Genocide". *Jacobin Magazine*.
https://www.jacobinmag.com/2019/09/white-genocide-great-replacement-theory.

[38] Another version of the same conspiracy theory, popular in Europe, goes by the name
of Kalergi Plan: Ward, J. (2018). "Day of the trope: White nationalist memes thrive
on Reddit's r/The_Donald". *Southern Poverty Law Center*. https://www.splcenter.org/
hatewatch/2018/04/19/day-trope-white-nationalist-memes-thrive-reddits-rthedonald.

in the slogans written on his weapons, he referred to both Lane's and Camus' ideas.[39]

While explicitly referencing several concepts from the conspiracy theories above, Tarrant's Manifesto was, however, a more stratified text than a simple espousal of right-wing anxieties about immigration. According to far-right radicalization expert Robert Evans,[40] the sprawling text was written with a series of layered references and intentions, in typical troll style (Nagle 2017), in order to provoke a reaction in the media and to inspire potential copycats by signaling his familiarity to the 4chan and 8chan subcultures. Tarrant manifesto and his communications via social media were thus addressed to two types of intended audience. At one level, they were meant to be read and absorbed by the media, together with other elements of his 'media-friendly' violent actions, such as the Facebook Live streaming, which added to his violent rampage an immersive quality typical of first-person shooter videogames. The first part of the manifesto is structured as a mock interview, presumably to provide media with soundbites to be widely distributed. However, unlike the densely theoretical terrorists' manifesto of the past, in his document Tarrant inserted several jokes, with the goal of stoking controversy and sparking media curiosity, but also of disguising his messages under a layer of irony that would cast doubt on its reliability and the seriousness of his political action.

Tarrant's crafting of this part of the manifesto mirrors the on-line practice of 'shitposting,' typical also of alt-right communications (Marwick and Lewis 2017; Singer and Brooking 2018), which consists of spreading "content, most of it ironic, low-quality trolling, for the purpose of provoking an emotional reaction in less Internet-savvy viewers" and to

---

[39] While originated in France, the Great Replacement ideological trope has now become global and influences American far-right movements as well. During the 2017 Charlottesville rally *Unite the Right*, which was marked by widespread violence, including the killing of a young woman protesting the rally, people could be heard singing 'You will not replace us' and 'Jews will not replace us', which refer to both Camus' and Lane's ideas. See Chatterton Williams, T. (2017). "The French origins of 'you will not replace us'". *The New Yorker*. https://www.newyorker.com/magazine/2017/12/04/the-french-origins-of-you-will-not-replace-us.

[40] Evans, R. (2019). "Shitposting, inspirational terrorism, and the Christchurch Mosque Massacre". *Bellingcat*. https://www.bellingcat.com/news/rest-of-world/2019/03/15/shitposting-inspirational-terrorism-and-the-christchurch-mosque-massacre/.

"to derail productive discussion and distract readers."[41] Among the references to the imageboard subculture, Tarrant included the well-known textual meme 'Navy Seal copypasta'[42] in the mock self-interview. Such meme was targeted at imageboards members, but it was also meant to trick journalists, so that they would mistakenly believe the attacker to be a former Navy Seal. In the manifesto, Brenton also credits American right-wing personality Candace Owens with beginning his radicalization. While Owens has championed anti-immigration positions, this statement was certainly meant to troll the media, since it was followed by Tarrant claiming that the videogame Spyro the Dragon 3 taught him ethnonationalism. This could be interpreted as responding to an established practice among *anons*,[43] or members of 4chan and 8chan, to troll or provoke the media for the sake of the *lulz* (Phillips 2015).

At a deeper level, however, the ironic parts of the manifesto were also meant to be received, both as a source of inspiration and as a set of codes signaling subcultural affiliation, by a global network of trolls, alt-right and far-right sympathizers. According to Evans, some of the content of the manifesto acted as bait "to draw the attention of his real intended audience."[44] Ambiguity and irony are a common rhetorical strategy in the discourse of far-right activists, as proudly claimed by alt-right poster boy and provocateur Milo Yiannopoulos (Cosentino 2017). Before leaving the car to enter the mosque and commit multiple murders, Tarrant could be heard saying "Remember lads, subscribe to PewDiePie," which is another reference to a 4chan and 8chan jargon. His ironic yet disruptive strategy is rendered obvious in this particular passage from the manifesto, where he calls on people who share his view to stir conflict by means of ambiguous tactics: "Place posters near public parks calling for sharia law, then in the next week place posters over such posters calling for the expulsion of all immigrants, repeat in every area of public life until the crisis arises." This post-truth approach to subversive political action echoes the manipulative

---

[41] Ibid.

[42] "Navy Seal Copypasta (…) is a facetious message containing a series of ridiculous claims and grandiose threats that portray the poster as an Internet tough guy stereotype". See https://knowyourmeme.com/memes/navy-seal-copypasta.

[43] The word is an abbreviation of the word anonymous, since the vast majority of the posts are by anonymous users.

[44] Evans (2019).

tactics originally conceptualized by Surkov in Russia and employed by the IRA during the 2016 US elections, as discussed in Chapter 2.

Tarrant thus appears to have crafted the perfect terrorist political manifesto of the post-truth era, skillfully tiptoeing a fine line between a radical fascist ideology and ironic jokes, between real threats and fictional elements, just like a Joker-type figure that entertains his fans and the media while committing hideous crimes. In the aftermath of the attack, the mainstream media channels, as well the main social media platforms, made several efforts not to publicize the attacker's Facebook video nor his manifesto, in order to limit the possibilities of copycats. Tarrant, however, had made sure that his intended audience had received it in advance. On March 15, 2019, just before the events in Christchurch, an anonymous message—most likely submitted by Tarrant himself—was posted to 8chan's /pol/board announcing an attack, which was to be livestreamed on Tarrant's Facebook page, as well as links to several copies of the manifesto uploaded to different web sites.

In the post, Tarrant declared his intention to move from 'shitposting' to 'effort posting,' which in the anon parlance means resorting to actual actions in real life. The post also encouraged other members of the imageboard in spreading Tarrant's message by means of "memes and shitposting," that is in the same semi-serious style of communications used by Tarrant and by the broader imageboard subculture. In the manifesto, Tarrant also encourages to "Create memes, post memes, and spread memes" claiming that "Memes have done more for the ethno-nationalist movement than any manifesto."[45] This statement explains why Tarrant's manifesto was full of memetic references, and reveals its belief that the most effective forms of inspiration and mobilization for on-line activists are memes and other elements of Internet popular culture. The validity of Tarrant belief in memetic warfare (Singer and Brooking 2018) is corroborated by the imageboards' reactions to the Christchurch attack. According to Evans, *anons* generally responded with enthusiasm to the actions and antics of Tarrant, celebrating them on 8chan as the achievement by one of them: "The shooter's frequent use of in-jokes and memes played extremely well with this crowd. (…) The shooter seems to have achieved his goal of providing the anons of 8chan with lulz, and with inspiration" (Evans 2019).

---

[45] Tarrant, B. (2019). *The great replacement* (p. 57). http://tarrantmanifesto.com/.

According to his own declaration in the manifesto, Tarrant became radicalized as a far-right terrorist two years prior to his attack in Christchurch. During a number of travels to various European countries in 2016 and 2017, in the aftermath of multiple ISIS-inspired attacks to European cities, he became particularly concerned with the threat of Islamic fundamentalism in the West. He also had become fascinated with the Balkan tradition of anti-Muslim sentiment, and with the history of the Balkan wars of resistance against the Ottoman Empire. Many of the weapons used by Tarrant during the attacked had been marked with references to famous historical episodes of such history.[46]

By his own admission in the manifesto, the Christchurch attacker drew also inspiration from Norwegian far-right terrorist Anders Breivik[47]—who in 2011 killed 77 people in two separate attacks against government offices and against the Labour Party Youth Association—adding that he had received approval for his actions from people affiliated with Breivik. The 2015 Charleston attack against African-American churchgoers committed by Dylan Roof was also cited as a source of inspiration for Tarrant. More recently, the ideological and communication elements of the Christchurch attack worked as a template for other attacks, including the 2019 El Paso shooting. The El Paso mass killer, Patrick Wood Crusius, had also posted a manifesto on 8chan, in which he echoed many of the same grievances and beliefs expressed by Tarrant, including reference to the Great Replacement conspiracy theory. The most recent sequence of violent actions by White ethnonationalists seems to present a pattern in the functioning of their radical politics, with imageboards and other fringe on-line venues serving as platform of radicalization, ideological support and inspiration that travel across borders, and memes and conspiracy theories serving as a common language and discourse (Davey and Ebner 2019). As conspiracy theories based on White identity politics increasingly circulate on-line, they go beyond being an American or European

[46] One of the rifles also bore the inscription 'Kebab removed'. See Al Jazeera. (2019). "Mosque shooter brandished material glorifying Serb nationalism". *Al Jazeera*. https://www.aljazeera.com/news/2019/03/zealand-mosque-gunman-inspired-serb-nationalism-190315141305756.html.

[47] "Breivik had shown to be inspired by massacres of Muslims in the Balkans in his 1500-page manifesto published prior to his mass shooting. In his manifesto, Breivik called Karadzic an 'honourable crusader'". Ibid.

political narrative and become a "call to arms to protect what is seen as the white race on a transnational level."[48]

The radicalization of the attacker in El Paso also happened in the 8chan/pol board, and an element of 'gamification' has been observed in the communications around the Christchurch, as well as in the El Paso and Pittsburgh attacks.[49] Among far-right activists and imageboards trolls, a kind of contest aimed at surpassing the body count of previous attacks started to become popular. The game-like quality of on-line conspiracy theory such as QAnon and the Great Replacement, and their violent escalation in real life, seems to be a common thread in the subcultural milieu of imageboards, where ironic layers, playful attitudes and radical political intentions are often intermixed.

Many observers also noted a parallel between the rhetoric of populist leaders such as Donald Trump,[50] who started his presidential campaign in 2016 stoking fears around an alleged invasion of Mexican immigrants with criminal intentions to the United States, and the xenophobic discourse common to the perpetrators of violent attacks in the name of the Great Replacement ideology. Several right-wing politicians and far-right movements have piggybacked on the anti-immigration wave that has swept across the Europe since 2015 and 2016, in the aftermath of the massive exodus of Syrian refugees fleeing from ISIS and Russian aerial bombings. The radical American ethnonationalists who have supported Donald Trump, led by self-styled ideologues such as Richard Spencer, are increasingly aligned with the positions of xenophobic right-wing populism that has surged in many parts of Europe. As radical ideas and beliefs against immigration have gained more traction and media coverage, the defense of European or Western ethno-culture that appears in many of the manifestos of far-right terrorists is becoming a mainstream political theme. The politically ambiguous concept of defending a common cultural heritage is then used as a justification for legitimizing ideas that are at their core dubiously close to racism and hate speech.

[48] Schwartzburg, R. (2019). "The 'white replacement theory' motivates alt-right killers the world over". *The Guardian*. https://www.theguardian.com/commentisfree/2019/aug/05/great-replacement-theory-alt-right-killers-el-paso.

[49] Evans (2019).

[50] Berger, J. M. (2018). "Trump is the glue that binds the far right". *The Atlantic*. https://www.theatlantic.com/ideas/archive/2018/10/trump-alt-right-twitter/574219/.

Such surge of ethnonationalist politics across multiple Western countries, as well as in the United States, appears to dovetail with the renewed Russian nationalism infused with religious and messianic references promoted by Putin under the guidance of Volodin. Putin's ambitions for a Russian political and cultural hegemony over Europe, and more broadly over the Western world, is now openly predicated on the defense of Christian heritage and values (Engström 2014). Of course, such strategy also results from Russia's ambitions to regain prominence and to challenge American global dominance. The allegations of connections between the American far-right movements and conservative Russian ideologues and politicians,[51] the already discussed accusations of collusion of the Trump campaign with Russian officials and the evidence of interference of the Russian government in the 2016 elections unearthed by the investigation of the US Department of Justice seem all to fall within a broader strategy by the Russian government to extend its sphere of geopolitical influence by relying on its appeal to a Christian conservative ideology challenging the moral and political relativism of liberal multiculturalism.

Tarrant's critique of the Western liberal democratic order appears to be genuinely rooted in his radical worldview and belief system, which fits with the Russian critique of Western liberal democracy. Identifying the culprit for the current state of social, political and environmental disarray, in his manifesto Tarrant speaks of a "mainstream, 'multicultural,' egalitarian, individualistic insanity" caused by liberal democracy and market capitalism. The suggested solution is to accelerate the crisis by means of "further polarizing Western society," another point that mirrors the Russian interference strategies to undermine the American democratic process discussed in the previous chapter. When arguing for the necessity of "radical, violent change," Tarrant mentions the philosophy of 'accelerationism,' originally proposed by British scholar Nick Land as a political approach to human and social progress based on speeding up economic and technological change and embracing the most destabilizing tendencies of capitalism.[52]

---

[51] Hawk, B. (2019). "Why far-right nationalists like Steve Bannon have embraced a Russian ideologue". *The Washington Post*. https://www.washingtonpost.com/outlook/2019/04/16/why-far-right-nationalists-like-steve-bannon-have-embraced-russian-ideologue/.

[52] Full automation of the production processes and the merging of human and technological dimensions are also advocated as necessary and inevitable for progress. Accelerationism, particularly the strand espoused by Mark Fisher, one of Land's students, has been

A darker, more subversive strand of the original Land idea has found warm reception among far-right movements across the world. This version of accelerationism aims at exacerbating existing social and political conflicts in order to undermine the foundations and the fabric of democracy, with the goal of establishing White ethno-states devoid of immigrants. This type of right-wing accelerationism, also known as 'darkcel,' is the political philosophy echoed by Tarrant in his manifesto, where he argues: "Stability and comfort are the enemies of revolutionary change. Therefore, we must destabilize and discomfort society wherever possible.(...)" through actions such as "voting for political candidates that radically change or challenge entrenched systems, radicalizing public discourse by both supporting, attacking, vilifying, and exaggerating all societal conflicts and attacking or even assassinating weak or less radical leaders/influencers on either side of social conflicts."[53] Tarrant actions should thus be read through the ideological prism of right-wing accelerationism, which advocates violent actions as means to speed up the decline of Western liberal democracy, alongside other transformative events such as the Brexit and the Trump presidency. As observed by Andy Beckett on The Guardian, "The disruptive US election campaign and manic presidency of Donald Trump, and his ultra-capitalist, anti-government policies, have been seen by an increasing number of observers (...) as the first mainstream manifestation of an accelerationist politics."[54]

Even Tarrant's choice of weapons, including the use of the AR15 military-style assault rifle, was done with an accelerationist mind-set. His goal was to further elevate the status of such deadly and contested weapon—used in many recent mass shootings, including by Edgar Welch in his foray at Comet Ping Pong—as a polarizing wedge within the American debate on gun control. IRA trolls also pushed divisive content on the issue of gun rights in the United States with the same intention of Tarrant that is "to create conflict between the two ideologies within the United

embraced by some fringes of the European left as a political approach that could address the flaws of capitalism by reducing working hours through automation and addressing social conflict through the use of technology.

[53] Tarrant (2019, 77).

[54] Beckett, A. (2017). "Accelerationism: How a fringe philosophy predicted the future we live in". *The Guardian*. https://www.theguardian.com/world/2017/may/11/accelerationism-how-a-fringe-philosophy-predicted-the-future-we-live-in.

States on the ownership of firearms in order to further the social, cultural, political and racial divide."[55] Coherently with his admiration for the Balkan wars against the Ottoman, and against the Bosnian Muslim minority during the Yugoslav wars, Tarrant literally refers the "balkanization of the US" as one of the goals that he aims to achieve through his actions.

In his manifesto, Tarrant hints to a familiar aspiration in the rhetoric of contemporary far-right ethnonationalism, particularly in the United States, which is the fragmentation and the dissolution of the country as a unified federal entity. Such grandiose objective would cause two related consequences, desired by ethnonationalists, which are the decline in the global hegemony of the multicultural United States and the creation of a plurality of ethnically pure smaller nations, along the model pursued by Serbian nationalists during the 1900s Yugoslav wars. Such outcome "will not only result in the racial separation of the people within the United States ensuring the future of the white race on the North American continent, but also ensuring the death of the 'melting pot'."[56] The collapse of the American multiculturalism and the invocation of a race war is another recurring theme of the far-right discourse, and it is a direct reference to the *Turner's Diary*, a dystopian novel by White supremacist author William Luther Pierce, a seminal text in the tradition of the American far-right. The ideas of a race war and the collapse of the United States as necessary preconditions for the emergence of a White ethno-state as a post-America are 'apocalyptic fantasies'[57] frequently espoused also by Richard Spencer, the principal ideologue of the American alt-right.

3.5   Conclusions

The wave of far-right politics that that has swept across the United States and Europe in recent years has brought several conspiracy theories from the fringes of on-line subcultures to the center of mainstream political conversations. Conspiracy theories are not anymore marginal, niche discourses relegated to an inferior epistemic status, but have gained legitimacy as alternative explanations for social and political problems. Their

---

[55] Tarrant (2019, 9).

[56] Ibid., 57.

[57] Wilson, A. (2019). "Fear-filled apocalypses: The far-right's use of conspiracy theories". *Oxford Research Group*. https://www.oxfordresearchgroup.org.uk/blog/fear-filled-apocalypses-the-far-rights-use-of-conspiracy-theory.

popularity owes also to the expedient endorsement by demagogic politicians such as Donald Trump. After his own election to the US presidency, Trump has continued spreading conspiracy theories, including the allegation that Obama had wiretapped Trump's office inside the Trump Tower, or that three million people had voted illegally in 2016. It would not be far-fetched to argue that Trump has elevated conspiracy theories as founding elements of his political communication strategy. This signals that the conspiratorial ethos, out of which fictional narratives such as Pizzagate and QAnon have emerged, currently permeates political conversations across from the United States to Europe, with important global ramifications.

A worldview based on conspiracy theories or beliefs "implies a universe governed by design" (Barkun 2013), where all-powerful cabals scheme against the welfare of the majority, or against a weak or dispossessed minority. As belief systems, conspiracy theories mirror the same Manichean divisions that undergird the populist rhetoric, pitting a powerful elite against an innocent and subjugated population. Conspiracy theories, as suggested by Uscinski, encapsulate challenges to power by marginal or disposed groups. More broadly, they signal the existence of a power crisis. It is the crisis of political power and of its representative institutions, from the media to cultural-scientific institutions, that allows for marginal, unorthodox political narratives to breach into the public conversation. The crisis of the epistemic paradigms that have underpinned the functioning of the Western modernity package, consisting on the technocratic management of society and on the twin pillars of liberal democracy and free-market capitalism, has caused the collapse of a regime of truth and consequently allowed the rapid growth of regimes of post-truth, relying on conspiracy theories. People who have stopped trusting institutions adopt conspiracy theories as epistemic gateways to decipher and expose the inner logics of political power.

As Western democracies seem increasingly unable to offer effective solutions to world problems that become more urgent and graver—from environmental threats to widening economic inequality, from massive migration flows to terrorism—conspiracy theories allow their believers to have their fears assuaged by a simple explanation that identifies a culpable subject yet avoids questioning the dynamics of power at their core. They offer a simulation of political action and critique that offers gratification, escapism, entertainment and a sense of political identity, without really demanding profound inquiry and sustained struggle to effectively address political and social problems.

Most of the conspiracy theories surveyed in this chapter share the common theme of a globalist elite of liberal politicians that operates secretively to undermine the standing of Western countries and of people of White ethnicity. Conspiracy theories on this theme could be seen as a kind of popular narrative that disenfranchised White Westerners tell themselves to process their cultural and political crisis and exorcise their fear of an irreversible decline. Conspiracy theories thus offer simple recipes for explaining complex realities and give their proponents the consolation of seeing themselves as elect carriers of secret and repressed knowledge. For proponents of conspiracy theories, the marginal or fringe status of their knowledge reinforces the belief of being representatives of a marginalized worldview that rests in direct opposition with an epistemic and political status quo. In some cases, as we have seen with the Epstein affair, conspiracy theories do act as channels of suppressed truths, while, however, falling short of really engaging with the structural causes of scandals and injustices.

Barkun (2013) has observed that far-right ideologies often present a convergence between apocalyptic beliefs and conspiracy theories. QAnon and Great Replacement supporters share a paranoid streak that borders with the apocalyptic, envisioning a grand plot aimed at the annihilation of the White race or at the exploitation of innocent victims on a global scale. The apocalyptic and paranoid components of the on-line conspiracy theories draw on a vast milieu of sources of inspiration to identify its multiple culprits, from global financiers like George Soros to the LGBTQ community, from immigrants to feminists. Continuously reinventing themselves, as we saw from the evolution of Pizzagate into QAnon, conspiracy theories transform and adapt by relying tactically on disparate elements from political, cultural and quasi-scientific sources. Barkun calls this type of flexible, constantly changing conspiratorial attitude 'improvisational millennialism,' a type of do-it-yourself, game-like apocalyptic belief system that has conquered on-line communities like 4chan and has motivated people like Tarrant to resort to deadly terrorist actions, all while spreading memes and making jokes.

REFERENCES

Barkun, M. (2013). *A culture of conspiracy*. Berkeley: University of California Press.

Benkler, J. et al. (2018). *Network propaganda. Manipulation, disinformation, and radicalization in American politics*. Oxford, UK: Oxford University Press.

Bulut, E., & Yoruk, E. (2017). Digital populism: Trolls and political polarization of Twitter in Turkey. *International Journal of Communication, 11*, 4093–4117.

Cosentino, G. (2017). *L'era della post-verità. Media e populismi dalla Brexit a Trump*. Reggio Emilia: Imprimatur.

Davey, J., & Ebner, J. (2019). 'The Great Replacement': The violent consequences of mainstreamed extremism. London: Institute for Strategic Dialogue.

Engström, M. (2014). Contemporary Russian messianism and new Russian foreign policy. *Contemporary Security Policy, 35*(2), 356–379.

Evans, R. (2019). Shitposting, inspirational terrorism, and the Christchurch Mosque Massacre. *Bellingcat*. https://www.bellingcat.com/news/rest-of-world/2019/03/15/shitposting-inspirational-terrorism-and-the-christchurch-mosque-massacre/.

Harsin, J. (2015). Regimes of post truth, post politics, and attention economies. *Communication, Culture & Critique, 8*(2), 327–333.

Kalpokas, I. (2018). *A political theory of post-truth*. London: Palgrave Macmillan.

Marwick, A., & Lewis, R. (2017). *Media manipulation and disinformation online*. Data and Society Research Institute.

Nagle, A. (2017). *Kill all normies*. UK: Zero Books.

Neiwert, D. (2017). *Alt-America. The rise of the radical right in the age of Trump*. London: Verso.

Phillips, W. (2015). *This is why we can't have nice things. Mapping the relationship between online trolling and mainstream culture*. Cambridge, MA: MIT Press.

Singer, P., & Brooking, E. (2018). *Likewar. The weaponization of social media*. Boston: Houghton Mifflin Harcourt.

Tarrant, B. (2019). *The Great Replacement*. http://tarrantmanifesto.com/.

Uscinski, J. (2017). The study of conspiracy theories. *Argumenta*. https://doi.org/10.23811/53.arg2017.usc.

Woolley, S., & Howard, P. (2018). *Computational propaganda*. Oxford, UK: Oxford University Press.

CHAPTER 4

Post-truth Politics in Syria: 'Rumor Bombs' on the White Helmets

Abstract This chapter presents a case study based on the analysis of a disinformation campaign carried by the Syrian regime and its ally Russia against the search-and-rescue organization globally known as the White Helmets, who operate since 2014 in Syria's rebel-held areas. This case study on the Syrian Civil War shows how rumors, conspiracy theories and other post-truth narratives in support of the Assad regime were given amplification by Russian media and via social media by a group of self-styled independent journalists and social media influencers, as well as by political bots and sock-puppet accounts. Such manipulative and propagandistic efforts found a receptive audience in Western countries, where social media users actively shared or co-created misleading or fictional narratives in a cultural and political context characterized by public opinion radicalization and polarization.

Keywords White Helmets · Syria · Citizen journalism · Twitter · Propaganda · Russia

4.1   Introduction

As discussed in the previous chapters, post-truth functions and it is reproduced also because its condition is strategically exploited by State actors and foreign policy initiatives. The case study presented in this chapter

© The Author(s) 2020
G. Cosentino, *Social Media and the Post-Truth World Order*,
https://doi.org/10.1007/978-3-030-43005-4_4

illustrates this aspect of post-truth and it is based on the analysis of a disinformation campaign carried by the Syrian regime and its ally Russia by means of computational propaganda (Woolley and Howard 2018) and so-called rumor bombs (Harsin 2018) via social media against the search-and-rescue organization globally known as the 'White Helmets.'

The concept of rumor bomb is particularly useful for the sake of this analysis to understand the functioning of such disinformation campaign in the context of post-truth politics. Rumor bombs are weaponized rumors, circulating between the political and military spheres, which are often left intentionally ambiguous so that to generate a state of disorientation, which is a "structure of feeling at the core of post-truth" (Harsin 2018) and which in Syria was aptly manipulated by the Assad regime and by Russia. While rumors can spread spontaneously in a grassroots form, such as those that sparked Pizzagate, "rumors and similar truth claims come just as commonly from resource-rich political and economic actors" (Harsin 2015, 2).

This case study on the Syrian Civil War, focusing primarily on the latest stage of the conflict, after the 2015 Russian intervention, shows how rumor bombs, conspiracy theories and other post-truth narratives in support of the Assad regime were exploited and given amplification by Russian media and via social media by a group of bloggers, independent journalists, social media influencers, automated bot accounts, trolls and sock-puppet accounts.[1] Such manipulative and propagandistic efforts found a receptive audience in Western countries characterized by public opinion radicalization and polarization.

The crisis of authority of traditional journalism and the related rise of citizen journalism functioned also as important drivers of post-truth in the Syrian war. The use of amateur videos, social media and citizen journalism pioneered by the Syrian opposition generated an often propagandistic and emotional type of war coverage, which was later mimicked and put at the service of a counternarrative effort in support of the Syrian regime (Trombetta 2012). Such new forms of media manipulation and propaganda based on user-generated content (UGC) was later given

---

[1] A sock-puppet account is a fake on-line identity created for purposes of deception and manipulation.

global visibility by Russia, which intervened in the conflict to defend its major geopolitical stakes in the region.

The crisis of authority of Western journalistic sources is also linked to a broader trust crisis in Western democratic institutions, which enabled post-truth conversations on the Syrian war among vast segments of the Western public opinion. Russia further exploited such fraying of the Western publics on the topic and leveraged on the lack of trusted sources of coverage on the conflict to put forth its propaganda efforts aimed at exhausting and disorienting the international public attention. The 'de-factualization of reality' (Roudakova 2017) which developed in Russia's media and political context under Putin's three terms as president, as seen in Chapter 2, was later exploited to influence other parts of the world, including the Middle East.

The chapter opens by discussing the war of narratives on the 2011 Syrian uprising and the related strategies of mutual imitation by the Assad regime and the opposition in the use of new communication technologies. The analysis then moves to look into the broader Russian involvement in the war and its use of propaganda and hybrid warfare in order to alter the military course in support of the Assad regime, also taking advance of the crisis of authority in the Middle East suffered by Western media and political institutions. Lastly, the chapter delves in the case study on the White Helmets by focusing specifically in the disinformation campaign jointly launched by the Syrian regime and by Russia, and actively supported by a plurality of social media users, to target militarily and undermine the credibility of the humanitarian organization.

As already discussed in the previous chapters, post-truth differs from mere disinformation and propaganda insofar as it is a broader concept that includes also the role of the audience/users as well as the historical and political context within which it occurs. Such conceptualization of post-truth involves an active role of audiences, who co-produce narrative fictions to fulfill subjective emotional or ideological needs. Post-truth narratives in Syria functioned as 'truth-games' (Harsin 2018) to which social media users actively participate in order to appeal and engage with the different 'truth-markets' and ideological niches they belong to, from the far-right to the far-left of the political spectrum. This case study aims at providing important insights into the implications of social media use as a platform for post-truth communications in non-Western contexts, specifically in undemocratic regimes or under conditions of armed conflict.

4.2   THE REGIME VS THE UPRISING: CONFLICTING NARRATIVES AND PARALLEL STRATEGIES

If there was ever any consensus within the international community on the motives and goals of the 2011 Syrian uprising, it was destined to be short-lived.[2] At the beginning, there was widespread hope in Syria that the uprising could bring political change and garner international support. The dominant narrative both in the Middle East and among Western observers portrayed an oppressed Syrian population rebelling against a dictatorial regime that had ruled with an iron fist over the country for forty years, severely limiting its progress. This perspective on the uprising could be called, in the words of academic Bassam Haddad, 'the pure and consistent revolution narrative' (Haddad 2016). The Syrian government, however, attempted to impose a different narrative which presented the protests as the product of foreign powers meddling with internal politics with the goal of bringing on a regime change, similarly to what had happened with the 2003 American intervention in Iraq. The government also suggested that protesters and rebels were in fact affiliated with Salafi Jihadist groups with the goal of destroying the secular leadership of the Assad family. For Haddad, this was the 'external conspiracy' narrative.

Since the beginning of the uprising, it was hard for external observers to assess the validity of the two conflicting narratives. The chaotic conditions on the ground made the coverage of the war extremely dangerous for foreign journalists. Also, Syria is notorious for having one of the most repressive environments for freedom of the press, ranking among the most censored media systems in the world according to Reporters Without Borders.[3] In the early phase of the war, the regime's reluctance to allow journalists into Syria allowed for a simplified understanding of the motives and dynamics of the uprising. Also, the few journalists that

---

[2] According to most accounts, the uprising started with the peaceful protests of citizens against the arrest and torture of a group of adolescents who in March 2011 had spray-painted the walls of their school in the city of Daraa with graffiti invoking the demise of President Bashar Al Assad. The protests in Daraa, followed by similar rallies elsewhere in the country by large segments of the population, expressing discontent with government corruption and decades-old emergency laws, were met with forceful repression by the authorities. For a more detailed account of this episode, see Al Jazeera News. (2017). "The boy who started the Syrian war". *Al Jazeera*. https://www.aljazeera.com/programmes/specialseries/2017/02/boy-started-syrian-war-170208093451538.html.

[3] See the 2018 World Press Freedom Index https://rsf.org/en/ranking/2018.

were able to enter Syria in 2011 and 2012 operated as embedded with the government forces and thus were exposed to limited or distorted versions of the ongoing conflict. In other cases, journalists with little or no knowledge of Arabic had often to resort to second-hand accounts, making the information verification process more difficult.

Despite the media blackout surrounding the Syrian conflict that some journalists lamented (Trombetta 2013), the uprising and the civil war that ensued were, however, extensively covered by means of new technologies, in what has been called the first truly 'socially mediated' war of the current era (Lynch et al. 2014). In particular, the combination of videos captured via mobile phones by activists and citizens and circulated via video sharing services like YouTube became an essential source of information about the conflict, for both the pan-Arab and the international media and audiences.[4] In most cases, these videos were captured and curated by activists, with different levels of production values, distributed from a plurality of local media centers scattered around the country. This ability of citizens and activists to provide a direct and unfiltered coverage of the ongoing crisis fits into the broader trend of citizen journalism and UGC that became prominent among the Arab Spring movements (Sienkiewicz 2014).

Social media in Syria created the perception of unfiltered and spontaneous information flows, which in reality were often curated by media hubs within networks of regime supporters or opposition activists endowed with a gatekeeping function, as important as that of mainstream media. With respect to this, Sienkiewicz (2014) talks about the importance of an 'interpreter' tier, consisting of semi-professional on-line journalists, mediating between citizen journalists and mainstream media, suggesting that in fact in the Syrian war a three-tier mechanism in the circulation of UGC was at work.

Despite thorough verification by mainstream media, the outpouring of UGC made it difficult for international observers to assess the structural biases of the interpreter tiers and to frame their information with established journalistic criteria, as in some cases the videos were meant

---

[4] The Wall Street Journal defined the Syrian conflict as 'the first war waged on YouTube.' The video sharing platform claimed that only in the first year of war over one million videos were distributed. For more on this, see Kaylan, M. (2013). "Syrian conflict as seen through YouTube". *The Wall Street Journal*. https://www.wsj.com/articles/syria8217s-war-viewed-almost-in-real-time-1380305826.

to craft a particular narrative and had a clear propagandist intent, meant at either bolstering the government crackdown or recruiting supporters and attracting funding from foreign countries supportive of the uprising.[5] The difficulties of established journalism in Syria, coupled with the surge of new media in war coverage, allowed for the emergence of conflicting narratives that essentially made the Syrian Civil War the first post-truth conflict of the twenty-first century: emotional and often unverifiable information supplanted rigorous and factual reporting, and competing interpretations of the events clashed constantly for over eight years.

The Syrian regime attempted to contrast the activists' coverage of the uprising by opening a YouTube channel, in some cases editing the video previously circulated by activists in order to question their authenticity. When pan-Arab television networks such as Al Jazeera started to broadcast the activists' videos, giving unprecedented legitimation to citizen journalism, the pro-regime TV network *Al-Duniya* begun broadcasting amateur videos in order to capture the same aesthetic and immediacy of the opposition communications and challenge their versions on the events in the streets. This signals what scholars like Trombetta (2012) consider a strategy of mutual imitation between the regime and the activists in their use of both traditional and new media, a strategy that as we shall see has informed propaganda activities also in later phases of the war.

Social media such as Facebook also had an important role in mobilizing protesters and activists, and in sharing information and propaganda either pro or against the Assad regime. The regime had a twofold approach to controlling activists' communications via the social network: initially, it had restricted access to Facebook, but it later allowed it in order to control the flow of hostile information and "force anti-regime activities to come out into the open" (Trombetta 2012, 7). The regime also exploited Facebook as a propaganda channel, by creating a plurality of sock-puppet accounts to celebrate the Assad regime.

In general, the Syrian new media environment was less developed than its Egyptian and Tunisian counterpart,[6] and even the use of social media by activists was less well integrated and coordinated with the actions on

---

[5] It is worth pointing out that the harrowing images and videos of atrocities committed by rebels and Islamist fighters, circulated to attract support from the Gulf States, in some cases ended up harming the opposition cause, at least from a Western perspective (Lynch et al. 2014).

[6] In 2011, only one-fifth of the total Syrian population had Internet access (Trombetta 2012).

the ground. As a result, social media, just as the Syrian media in general, suffered a crisis of authority from the onset of the conflict, and protesters were less able to communicate their demands and document their suffering in a way that was reliable and verifiable. The Syrian new media environment thus became conducive to "overabundance of information, heightened polarization, the birth of digital enclaves isolated from one another, and the production of low quality content based on emotional images and data, rather than on rational texts and arguments" (Trombetta 2013, 48),[7] a description which reads strikingly prescient of the current definition of the post-truth condition.

For the sake of this analysis, the now eight years of conflict in the Syrian Civil War will be divided into three historical phases: an initial phase, between 2011 and 2013, during which the opposition factions, some of which supported by the United States, the UK, Qatar, Saudi Arabia and other foreign powers, made significant territorial gains; a second phase, between 2014 and 2015, characterized by the expansion of the so-called Islamic State, a Salafi Jihadist militant movement operating between Iraq and Syria[8]; and a third phase, after 2015, marked by the further radicalization of rebel groups with Islamist positions and by the surge in Russian military support to President Assad, with aerial campaigns in rebel-held areas which led to the regime regaining control over much the Syrian territory.

Each historical phase was characterized by a specific narrative with respect to the nature and the goals of the uprising and of the conflict that followed, according to the course of the military events on the ground. As with many contemporary conflicts, the narrative dimension of the war became an equally contested terrain as the actual physical dimension (Patrikarakos 2017), thus creating conditions for a blurring between

---

[7] Similar remarks are made in a report issued by the United States Institute of Peace, which detected a clustering into insular communities of like-minded Syrian activists and citizens, particularly on Twitter, without, however, taking the form of clear polarization but rather of a "complex web of multiple insular networks" (Lynch et al. 2014, 6).

[8] After 2012, the Assad regime gradually allowed Western journalists to visit the embattled areas, and a more complex reality about the war and its motives started to emerge. It became evident that the initial political objectives behind the uprising started to be supplanted by religious ones, as the conflict was becoming increasingly sectarian. It also became more difficult to unequivocally sustain the simplistic narrative of the first phase of the war, pitting a dictator against a peaceful uprising.

information and propaganda in the interplay between new media and traditional media coverage of the war, which is the particular aspect of post-truth under discussion in this chapter.

As the situation on the ground was growing increasingly complex, both sides were also conducting an intensifying conflict on-line, where information efforts morphed into overt propaganda and disinformation campaigns. Attempts by the Syrian government and its supporters to upset the dominant narrative around the uprising with disinformation were already visible in the initial period.[9] Such early phase of disinformation was local and spontaneous, with some coordination by the regime through a cyber-warfare outfit called Syrian Electronic Army. Rebel factions also resorted to spreading false information, often using the same footage depicting hideous crimes that the regime was circulating.[10]

Social media were also actively involved in spreading both propaganda and disinformation to shape the narratives around the conflict, with the emergence of Twitter wars characterized by violent and partisan discourse between critics and supporters of Bashar Al Assad, which continue to this day. Twitter was also turned into a terrain for cyberwarfare: in 2012, the Reuters news agency had its Twitter account hacked and used to distribute anti-opposition propaganda, an operation allegedly linked to the Syrian Electronic Army. The group, with close ties to President Assad,[11] adopted the strategy to target popular media outlets in order to spread disinformation in support of the regime or harmful to the opposition. The opposition was also involved in the spreading of rumors and false information via Twitter.[12]

---

[9] One particular video showed a captive being beheaded with a chainsaw, with both fronts in the conflict accusing the enemy of committing the atrocity, while the footage was in fact originally taken five years prior in Mexico during an execution of a rival by a local drug lord.

[10] Shelton, T. (2012). "The most disturbing fake videos making the rounds in Syria". *Public Radio International.* https://www.pri.org/stories/2012-11-12/most-disturbing-fake-videos-making-rounds-syria.

[11] Apps, P. (2012). "Disinformation flies in Syria's growing cyber war". *Reuters.* https://www.reuters.com/article/us-syria-crisis-hacking/disinformation-flies-in-syrias-growing-cyber-war-idUSBRE8760GI20120807.

[12] A famous example involved a Twitter account purporting to be that of a senior Russian official, suggesting that Assad had been murdered, which prompted the Russian Foreign Ministry to officially deny the information.

In general, following Trombetta (2013), one could observe in the early phase of the war an attempt by the regime to update its propaganda strategies by using new media and spreading amateur videos, either real or fake. On the other hand, activists attempted to establish themselves as a reliable news source in the eyes of mainstream media, despite the often propagandistic and highly emotional nature of their content. In their mutual efforts, both sides monitored and mimicked each other, and both contributing the exacerbation of the post-truth condition surrounding the Syrian conflict.

After 2014, when ISIS became the focus of international attention, the 'war on terror' trope used by the Syrian government to counter the opposition gradually started to materialize as the rebels became more closely affiliated with radical Islamist groups. The sudden rise of ISIS in the period between 2014 and 2015 had an unexpected and pivotal impact both on the military and on the symbolic dimension of the conflict, insofar as it shocked the main narrative of the early phase of war and broke it down into several conflicting perspectives and accounts, which eventually became instrumental to the regime counternarrative.

4.3   Russian Hybrid Warfare in Syria

The focus of this section is on the third and more recent phase of the Syrian war, which can be dated from late 2015 onward. In this period, the counternarrative promoted by the Syrian government, alleging the meddling of foreign powers in Syria and presenting opposition and rebel forces as terrorists with a radical religious agenda, has found increased backing by Russia authorities and media, and has been propagated by myriads of social media accounts, both real and automated, from various world regions.

Since the Russian authorities decided to directly intervene in the Syria conflict in September 2015, they have made propaganda as an integral part of their military campaign. As the Russia's actions in Syria were "cloaked in the guise of one of the twenty-first century's most sacred geopolitical tropes: fighting terrorism" (Patrikarakos 2017), the official goal of the military intervention was to counter the spread of ISIS. It, however, became immediately clear that the real objective was to prevent the fall of the Assad regime and to defeat the opposition forces, while at the same time taking advantage of the United States diminished status in the region to advance Russia's geopolitical stakes. Syria presented an opportunity for the Kremlin to further employ the so-called hybrid war-fare doctrine,[13] which was tested in the conflict in Georgia in 2008 and later successfully implemented in the 2014 war with Ukraine. The strategy implies the use of media manipulations tactics, including disinformation and cyberwarfare, to influence discourses and narratives in support of conventional or irregular warfare.[14]

The pro-Assad propaganda efforts in Syria after 2015 then resulted in a campaign to which Russia has lent its full arsenal of media influence, from its global all-news network RT to the on-line news agency Sputnik, all the way to a set of social media actors, some of which relatively unknown until recently, who have been elevated to the status of authority on the Syrian conflict by the Russian media. Following Sienkiewicz (2014) and Lynch et al. (2014), we could consider these actors as being an 'interpreter tier' that served an important gatekeeping function in filtering information being released as UGC and crafting with it a pro-regime narrative. Some of the most popular names among this influential group of pro-Assad opinion leaders are former *Salon* editor Max Blumenthal, Canadian activist Eva Bartlett, Twitter influencer such as Sarah Abdallah, who can count on a vast following despite having no record of journalistic activity and whose real identity is a matter of speculation,[15] and British independent journalist Vanessa Beeley, the daughter of a former British diplomat, who is a frequent contributor to RT and editor of the alternative news outlet twenty-first century Wire, founded by a former editor of the conspiracy theory-oriented web site Infowars.[16]

[13] Pomerantsev, P. (2014). "How Putin is reinventing warfare". *Foreign Policy*. https://foreignpolicy.com/2014/05/05/how-putin-is-reinventing-warfare.

[14] Alami, M. (2018). "Russia disinformation campaign has changed how we see Syria". *Atlantic Council*. http://www.atlanticcouncil.org/blogs/syriasource/russia-s-disinformation-campaign-has-changed-how-we-see-syria.

[15] According to a BBC report on pro-Assad influencers spreading disinformation on-line, Sarah Abdallah is presented as having "more than 125,000 followers, among them more than 250 journalists from mainstream media outlets. Her follower count is comparable to BBC journalists who regularly report on Syria. (…) She has almost no online presence or published stories or writing away from social media platforms". BBC News. (2018). "The online activists pushing Syria conspiracy theories". *BBC*. https://www.bbc.com/news/blogs-trending-43745629.

[16] It should be pointed out that prior to her support for the Assad regime, Beeley has publicly expressed her belief that 9/11 was not perpetrated by Al-Qaeda and that the Charlie Hebdo attack was staged. See York, C. (2018). "How an obscure british blogger became Russia's key witness against the White Helmets". *HuffingtonPost*.

While these activists or independent journalists often present themselves as anti-war, with some of them having in the past championed traditional leftist or pacifist causes such as Palestinian cause, they currently seem to share a supportive stance toward the military actions of the Syrian government and its Russian ally. Their perspective on the Syrian war is clearly based on the 'foreign plot' narrative, and clearly ideologically oriented with the geopolitical strategy of Russia, thus openly anti-American and anti-Nato. What is not clear is whether these influencers have a political or professional connection with the Russian government and thus knowingly circulate propaganda and disinformation, or rather spontaneously support pro-regime narratives, co-producing them with an 'aspirational' goal to advance their professional or political status (Kalpokas 2018). It is, however, proven that Beeley met with Assad and Maria Zakharova, the Director of the Department of Information and Press at the Ministry of Foreign Affairs of Russia,[17] and Blumenthal, who had originally supported the Syrian uprising, changed his views on the conflict after attending the celebrations for RT ten years anniversary in Moscow.[18]

As discussed by Sienkiewicz, independent journalists like James Miller and Eliot Higgins—the latter founder of the respected open-source journalism web site Bellingcat—played an important role during the early phase of the Syrian war in mediating between UGC and amateur videos and mainstream media. In the process, they helped uncover important evidence of the use of chemical weapons by the regime.[19] By empowering activists and journalists like Beeley and Bartlett, the Assad regime and Russia appear to have chosen to weaponize the growing legitimacy of UGC and citizens journalism in the context of the media coverage of the

Available at http://www.huffingtonpost.co.uk/entry/vanessa-beeley-syria-whitehelmets_uk_5ad9b6cae4b03c426dad48a9.

[17] Di Giovanni, J. (2018). "Why Assad and Russia target the White Helmets". *The New York Review of Books.* https://www.nybooks.com/daily/2018/10/16/why-assad-and-russia-target-the-white-helmets/.

[18] Hamad, S., & Oz, K. (2017). "Did a Kremlin pilgrimage cause AlterNet blogger's damascene conversion?" *Pulse.* https://pulsemedia.org/2017/08/22/did-a-kremlin-pilgrimage-cause-alternet-bloggers-damascene-conversion/.

[19] https://www.bellingcat.com/tag/chemical-weapons/.

Syrian conflict. A tier of social media interpreters and influencers was 'deployed' to match and counter the role of Higgins and other independent journalists who had stepped in to provide valuable verification and analysis of the wealth of data and material concerning the war, in the processing providing damning information against the regime.

A common element that characterizes the emergence of the counternarrative pushed forth by social media influencers in support of the Syrian regime is that it presents itself as being based on perspectives that are allegedly omitted or distorted in the Western mainstream media. This approach expediently relies on the rhetoric surrounding efforts of citizen journalism and UGC as champions of an adulterated 'vox populi,' and it mirrors the typical post-truth arguments supported by conspiracy theory proponents discussed in Chapter 3. The focus on these influencers is on revealing plots, schemes and machinations that political and media elites are covering up, and only 'independent' journalists dare to uncover. The stories and narratives promoted suggest that mainstream media and human rights organizations are covertly aligned with Western governments and Gulf States in a plot to topple the Syrian regime. While there might be some elements of truth, as in the CIA covert operation to fund and train rebel groups to fight in Syria, the opinions and reports are often cloaked in the paranoid and fictional discourse typical of conspiracy theorists and often lack factual evidence for their claims, as demonstrated by various fact-checking initiatives.

In this respect, such counternarrative parallel dynamics seen at work during the Trump and Brexit campaigns, where propaganda or disinformation efforts were presented as countering official media narratives, and populist politicians leveraged on public's mistrust of traditional parties and media to advance their contentious views. Conspiracy theories often rest at the core of the belief system of both right-wing and left-wing apologists of Assad, serving the function of simplifying complex political and military scenarios with identifiable scapegoats and culprits. The conspiracy theory-prone mind-set that frequently infuses the current political discourse in the United States and Europe has proved a fertile ground for seeding post-truth narratives that have been beneficial to Russian propaganda efforts, including in the Syrian war.

A well-known example of conspiracy theory in Syria is the argument that the chemical weapon attacks allegedly perpetrated by the regime were in fact so-called false flag operations carried by the rebels in order to prompt Western military intervention, a claim that is often reiterated, but without supportive evidence.[20] Interestingly, as discussed in the previous chapter, the 'false flag' trope is also one of the most frequent features in the discourse of the pro-gun on-line subculture and of the global White ethnonationalist community. Putin himself voiced this opinion in a 2013 op-ed on the New York Times.[21]

Since 2013, the United Nations has confirmed several incidents of chemical weapons use in the Syrian conflict, with the most well-known episodes being the Ghouta (2013), Khan Shaykhun (2017) and Douma (2018) attacks. The alleged use of chemical weapons against civilian targets has attracted international condemnation since 2013, and the UN investigators have reported on several occasions that the attacks had been carried by government forces.[22] A BBC investigation also confirmed the responsibility of the Assad regime in dozens of chemical attacks since 2013.[23] Western media reports on this matter have, however, been met with skepticism by sections of the international public opinion. The discredited *New York Times* articles about the alleged stockpile of chemical weapons possessed by the Saddam Hussein regime, which was used as a justification for the ill-fated US intervention of Iraq in 2003, are of course a damning precedent which has made people especially skeptical on this matter. Such notorious journalistic blunder by an established legacy media institution has become the source and the justification for chemical weapons 'denialism' in the Syrian war. Such type of denialism is another post-truth feature of the discourses around Syria, and it has stoked the

[20] See Mackey, R. (2018). "Russia says it has 'irrefutable evidence' U.K. staged chemical attack in Syria. Let's see it". *The Intercept.* https://theintercept.com/2018/04/13/russia-says-its-irrefutable-evidence-chemical-attack-syria-staged-lets-see/; Palma, B. (2018). "Disinformation and conspiracy trolling in the wake of the Syrian chemical attack". *Snopes.* https://www.snopes.com/news/2018/04/12/disinformation-conspiracy-trolling-syrian-chemical-attack/; Gillin, J. (2017). "Conspiracy claims that Syrian gas attack was 'false flag' are unproven". *Politifact.* https://www.politifact.com/truth-o-meter/article/2017/apr/07/unproven-online-theories-doubting-syrian-gas-attac/.

[21] Putin, V. (2013). "A plea for caution from Russia". *The New York Times.* https://www.nytimes.com/2013/09/12/opinion/putin-plea-for-caution-from-russia-on-syria.html.

[22] Nebehay, S. (2018). "U.N. documents further Syrian government use of banned chemical." *Reuters.* https://www.reuters.com/article/us-mideast-crisis-syria-warcrimes/u-n-documents-further-syrian-government-use-of-banned-chemical-weapons-idUSKCN1LS1JH.

[23] Al-Maghafi, N. (2018). "How chemical weapons have helped Assad". *BBC News.* https://www.bbc.com/news/world-middle-east-45586903.

belief in conspiracy theories and prevented any attempt by the international community to hold the Assad regime accountable on the use of chemical weapons.

Another example of disinformation related to chemical weapons is the #SyriaHoax Twitter campaign which followed the April 2017 Khan Shaykhun chemical attack, when the sarin nerve agent was dropped on a civilian area. The attack caused nearly a hundred deaths, a third of them children, and it was followed by a series of retaliatory missile strikes ordered by the Trump administration against a military base of the Syrian army. The missile attacks prompted the fear of a US military intervention in Syria, one of the long-standing arguments used by Assad supporters to warn against the renewed threat of US imperialism and military expansionism in the Middle East. After a pro-Assad newspaper in Lebanon circulated the rumor that the sources on the ground confirming the Sarin attack were dubious, the Russian propaganda machine amplified it across multiple platforms, including the Twitter accounts of various Russian embassies. A network of social media accounts and bots, allegedly affiliated by the Russian propaganda outfit IRA,[24] started to spread the narrative that the attack didn't happen and that the opposition forces had either staged it or perpetrated to prompt retaliatory measures by Western powers.

The 'false flag' narrative frame was used by the global community of Assad supporters, both in the Middle East and in the United States. The hashtag #SyriaHoax was promoted by Russian trolls and political bots on social media and various discussion groups and web sites popular among the US alt-right community, and a day after the retaliatory missile attack by the Trump administration the #SyriaHoax was the number one trending Twitter topic in the United States. A study from the advocacy group The Syria Campaign, which supports the Syrian opposition, found that the Russian and Syrian propaganda reached a wider audience than did the mainstream media coverage of the attack (The Syria Campaign 2017). Infowars, notorious for peddling conspiracy theories, also called the Khan Shaykhun attack a 'false flag' operation meant to provide justification for the US missile strike and for a plot to bring down Assad. In October

[24] Ross, B., et al. (2017). "Behind #SyriaHoax and the Russian propaganda onslaught". *ABC News*. https://abcnews.go.com/International/analysts-identify-syriahoax-russian-fueled-propaganda/story?id=46787674.

2017, experts from the OPCW-UN Joint Mission in Syria expressed confidence that the Syrian Air Force had dropped the chemical weapons at Khan Shaykhun, but such official statement didn't displace the false flag narrative from the public conversation.

4.4 'Dismiss, Distort, Distract, Dismay': Russia's Strategy Against the White Helmets

The case study in this section focuses on a propaganda campaign via social media that has targeted the humanitarian search-and-rescue organization Syria Civil Defense, globally known as the White Helmets.[25] The White Helmets were founded in 2013 by James Le Mesurier, a British army veteran, as a response to the lack of institutional resources for the protection of civilian population affected by the conflict in the areas of Aleppo and Idlib outside of government control. Since the 2015 Russian military intervention, the humanitarian group has provided aid in the immediate aftermath of aerial bombardments by the Syrian and Russian Air Force. Operating out of 120 centers, the group consists of nearly 3500 people, largely coming from civil society, who receive a modest salary and training thanks to the funding by Western countries, including the United States, the UK, Japan and Turkey.[26] The White Helmets—who claim to have saved nearly a hundred thousand people since the beginning of the war— were the subject of an Academy Award-winning documentary in 2017, were nominated twice for the Nobel Prize and received several awards and accolades for their humanitarian work. While the White Helmets claim to be an independent and impartial humanitarian NGO, without affiliation to political or military actions, they are, however, considered to be supportive of the opposition by some international observers (Atlantic Council 2017).

Starting in 2016, shortly after Russian intervention in Syria, the White Helmets have been subject to what several Western media outlets including the BBC, *The Guardian*, France 24 and think tanks like the Atlantic Council consider a sustained disinformation campaign based on 'rumor

---

[25] The nickname comes after the signature white headgear they wear.

[26] The sources of funding are disclosed by the group on their web site http://syriacivildefense.org.

bombs' (Harsin 2018) relying on all the resources of the Russian and pro-Assad propaganda arsenal. The Russian disinformation campaign against the White Helmets followed the so-called 4D approach identified by an Atlantic Council report as the guiding strategy of all media manipulation tactics employed by Kremlin in support of its military actions in Syria: "Dismiss the critic, distort the facts, distract from the key point, and dismay the audience" (Czuperski et al. 2016). In this section, I will analyze the disinformation campaign by discussing the four components suggested by the Atlantic Council.

As for the first component—dismissing the critic—the main reason for targeting the White Helmets from both a symbolic and military perspective is that the group often provide documentation of the consequences of the Russian and Syrian regime aerial bombing campaigns. The members of the organization wear body cameras and provide footage of the destruction caused by air strikes against civilian infrastructures and population, which is often posted on social media, thus emerging as an essential source of evidence of alleged war crimes. In lack of independent and reliable journalistic accounts from mainstream media on the frontline, and in continuity with the role of activists in the coverage of the conflict discussed at the beginning of the chapter, the humanitarian organization has filled a gap by providing evidence portraying the human cost of the military offensive to regain rebel-held areas. As it had been since the beginning of the conflict, the role of UGC remains a key element in its coverage, particularly in challenging the regime narratives, thus becoming an essential target for a counter-information strategy.

During the final phase of the Aleppo siege, in the fall of 2016, despite the denial by Russian authorities, the White Helmets recorded the use of barrel bombs and cluster munitions, which had been banned by a UN resolution in 2014. In 2017, the White Helmets provided also crucial evidence to the UN body in charge of investigating the use of chemical weapons in the Khan Shaykhun attack.[27] According to an investigation by *The Guardian*, the footage by the White Helmets has helped human rights organizations such as Amnesty and the Syria Justice and Accountability Center to verify and support testimony from people in Syria about the targeting of schools and hospital by the aerial campaigns.

---

[27] Di Giovanni, J. (2018). "Why Assad and Russia target the White Helmets". *The New York Review of Books*. https://www.nybooks.com/daily/2018/10/16/why-assad-and-russia-target-the-white-helmets.

The White Helmets provided essential information and evidence to the critics of the Russian intervention in Syria, upsetting the Syrian and Russian narrative on the goal of their military campaign. As such, the White Helmets were targeted and dismissed as an unreliable or biased source of criticism.[28] The targeting of the White Helmets was part of a broader hybrid warfare strategy that included 'double tap' aerial bombing, whereby a target is hit twice at short distance between each attack. This proved particularly deadly and effective in neutralizing the immediate humanitarian efforts of first responders to the victims. As a result, the number of volunteers wounded or killed in rescue operations has risen significantly since 2016.[29]

As far as distorting the facts, the second component of the strategy, the main goal of the disinformation campaign was to portray the humanitarian organization as linked to Jihadist militants and terrorist groups, thus a potential military target undeserving of humanitarian protection. This is the most obvious instance of targeting the group with 'rumor bombs,' and it was couched into the 'war on terror' narrative consistently pursued by the regime since 2011 and by Russia after 2015. Pro-Assad news outlet *Hands Off Syria*, Russian officials and Kremlin-backed media such as RT have accused the White Helmets of working with the Al-Qaeda-affiliated Al-Nusra Front. As it is often the case in the Syrian conflict, amateur photos, videos and other UGC from sources difficult to verify were often used as evidence to back up these claims. High-level Russian institutions such the Russian Embassy in the UK have been involved in the campaign too, by spreading memes on Twitter alleging White Helmets' connection with terrorists, showing how 'memetic warfare' has been adopted also by institutions. Russian delegates to the UN security council and to the UN general assembly presented a paper written by Vanessa Beeley,[30] who

---

[28] According to an Atlantic Council Report "Between August 13th and December 31st, 2016, Russian News Agency Sputnik ran twenty-seven articles that mentioned the White Helmets. Of those, twenty-four were negative, two were neutral, and just one—a preview of the Nobel Peace Prize contenders—was positive" (Atlantic Council 2017, 59).

[29] As of 2019, over 200 White Helmets have died in their effort to provide humanitarian relief, despite being protected by International Humanitarian law.

[30] Vanessa Beeley has also been indicated by researchers as dominating the online conversation around the White Helmets, and while presenting herself as independent, her connection with the Kremlin has been widely documented. See Solon, O. (2017). "How Syria's White Helmets became victims of an online propaganda machine".

went to Syria for the first time only in 2016, criticizing the White Helmets and linking them to Al-Qaeda. A thorough France 24 investigation has either declared unproven or debunked these claims, while, however, reporting that in several occasions the White Helmets had to negotiate with armed Islamist groups in order to operate in the territories under their control. The ambiguity of the claims against the White Helmets was, however, enough to make the rumor bomb effective and to make it circulate widely via social media as memes and other forms of weaponized Internet entertainment (Singer and Brooking 2018).[31]

In another example of rumor bomb, the White Helmets were also accused of staging their reports on civilian casualties or even fabricating evidence of chemical attacks to cater to Western media, audience and policymakers. Such allegations have come directly from Russian Foreign Minister Sergey Lavrov and from Russian Ministry of Defense spokesman Konashenkov, who accused Unicef of "falling victim to another hoax by the White Helmets."[32] In a speech organized by the Syrian mission at the UN, Eva Bartlett, who also writes for *RT*, alleged that the White Helmets staged their rescues by using recycled victims, a claim that originated as a meme, and that Lavrov repeated, and that eventually was debunked by *Channel 4 News*.[33] Social media influencer Sarah Abdallah was one of the most vocal critics of the White Helmets, accusing them of fabrications and voicing her criticism to a pro-Assad information ecosystem populated by "supporters of pro-Palestinian causes, Russians and Russian

The Guardian. https://www.theguardian.com/world/2017/dec/18/syria-white-helmets-conspiracy-theories.

[31] France 24. (2018). "White Helmets collaborating with terrorists? We sort fact from fiction (part 1)". *France 24*. https://observers.france24.com/en/20180510-syria-white-helmets-terrorists-fact-fiction-islamic-state.

[32] Sputnik. (2016). "Russia registered US attack drone in area where Idlib school was attacked—MoD". *Sputnik*. https://sputniknews.com/middleeast/201610271046810904-idlib-school-russia.

[33] Worrall, P. (2016). "FactCheck: Eva Bartlett's claims about Syrian children". *Channel 4 News*. https://www.channel4.com/news/factcheck/factcheck-eva-bartletts-claims-about-syrian-children.

allies, white nationalists and those from the extremist alt-right, conservative American Trump supporters, far-right groups in Europe and conspiracy theorists."[34] This varied ideological front presents many points in common with the on-line communities identified in the previous chapters and responsible for the global circulation of ethnonationalist or anti-Muslim conspiracy theories.

The communication efforts by Assadist influencers and Russian agents in the Syrian conflict consisted in the dissemination of pro-regime narratives among different segments of the Western audience, from the far-left to the far-right, in order to generate a complex and confusing discourse on the war which would hinder international consensus and stall policymaking. As a result, Assad has gained near cult status in some circles of the US alt-right and European far-right, as well as of the far-left. This is a further indication of how easily post-truth narratives circulate among interconnected global subcultures with strong ideological orientation, a dynamic also observed in the previous chapter. Both right-wing and left-wing supporters of President Assad also share the same anti-interventionist stance with respect to possible retaliatory measures by the West to punish the alleged war crimes by the Syrian regime. Such anti-war stance is, however, partial, and it is not equally applied toward the Russian intervention in the opposition areas controlled by Syrian rebels and Jihadist militias.

The support to Assad is not limited to fringe political circles. In the United States, former presidential candidate Jill Stein voiced her support for the Syrian regime, and in the UK, Labour Party leader Jeremy Corbyn had publicly refused to blame Assad for chemical weapons attack.[35] Also, Corbyn supporters on Twitter often provide amplification to the views of Assadist influencers such as Vanessa Beeley. The support to Assad by important segments of the most ideologically aligned and radical sections of the Western public opinion is a further indicator of the declining

---

[34] It was this variegated group, similar to other on-line social formations peddling conspiracy theories as seen in Chapter 3, that pushed the #SyriaHoax hashtag to trending in 2017. See BBC News (2018).

[35] See Reid Ross, A. (2018). "How Assad's war crimes bring far left and right together—Under Putin's benevolent gaze". *Haaretz*. https://www.haaretz.com/middle-east-news/assad-s-war-crimes-bring-far-left-and-right-together-and-putin-smiles-1.6008713; Culthorpe, T. (2018). "Corbyn refuses to blame Assad for chemical attack in Syria". *Daily Mail Online*. https://www.dailymail.co.uk/news/article-5594765/Corbyn-refuses-blame-Assad-chemical-attack-Syria.html.

trust in Western democracies' role in the Middle East and of the already discussed fraying of the Western public opinion along irreconcilable positions. All of these elements together further contributed to the post-truth drift taken by the conversation and discourse on the Syrian war.

A further accusation against the White Helmets claims that they are funded by foreign powers with the covert intention of bringing on a regime change in Syria. The funding that the White Helmets publicly disclose, coming mainly from the UK through the Conflict, Stability and Security Fund, as well as other Western countries, is thus used as a proof that they have an agenda and that the evidence they provide on the war cannot be trusted. After the Khan Sheikhoun chemical attack, Infowars went as far as to accuse the White Helmets of being an "al-Qaida affiliated group funded by George Soros."[36] Accusing somebody of having an alleged 'Soros connection,' which can also be considered another instance of rumor bombing, is a recurring trope in the conspiratorial rhetoric and discourse of far-right and populist media. The White Helmets, however, have never received funding from George Soros or any of his foundations.

While some of the accusations leveled have in fact being proven correct or at least not disprovable, like the already mentioned frequent contacts between the White Helmets and some rebel Islamist groups, or the accusations that some members of the group carry arms, the most serious allegations have been found baseless by various fact-checking investigations,[37] particularly those carried by the BBC, *The Guardian*, France 24, Channel 4 News and by fact-checking web sites such as Snopes.[38] However, as seen in other case studies, and as theorized by Harsin, the fact-checking and debunking efforts have had little success in preventing the further spreading of these rumors, since these are confined to insular communities that are impervious to contradicting information and external scrutiny of their beliefs.

The distortion of the facts on the White Helmets, the rumor bombing against them by labeling them as terrorists and the allegations of staged chemical attacks, helped reach also the third goal of the Russian counternarrative strategy, which was the distraction of the public opinion from

---

[36] Solon (2017).

[37] France 24 (2018).

[38] See   https://www.snopes.com/fact-check/syrian-rescue-organization-the-white-helmets-are-terrorists/.

the key point of the Russian intervention: the military support to the Syrian regime to regain territory and crush the opposition forces. By dismissing key evidence and witnesses of the dramatic consequences on civilians of their aerial bombing campaign, Russian and Syrian authorities were able to deceive the public opinion about their military ends. Through an outpouring of coordinated content circulated by bots, trolls and sockpuppet accounts, and by giving wide media exposure to a network of influencers, agitators and propagandists, Russian and Syrian authorities have been able to create a manufactured consensus on the White Helmets and to give fringe contentious views mainstream visibility and legitimacy.

The analytics firm Graphika, specialized in the study of Russian disinformation campaigns, found similar patterns in the on-line ecosystem created by thousands of Twitter users talking about the White Helmets. Among these users, there were pro-Kremlin accounts, generating in some cases over hundred tweets per day, which is typically an indicator of a bot account. Only on Twitter, an army of social media accounts and bots has been able to reach an "estimated 56 million people with tweets attacking (…) the White Helmets during ten key moments of 2016 and 2017."[39] Social media and search engine algorithms have also been exploited so that damaging content against the White Helmets could appear at the top of search results on Google or YouTube.[40]

The notion of the White Helmets as an alleged terrorist organization seems to have entered the mainstream conversation and reached a wide audience, as it was also publicly circulated by Pink Floyd co-founder Roger Waters, who during a 2018 concert accused the humanitarian organization of being "a fake organization that exists only to create propaganda for the jihadists and terrorists."[41] It thus became evident that the fourth component of the Russian disinformation audience, dismaying the audience and stoking fears and confusion, had also been achieved.

The White Helmets were also not immune to mistakes, which have provided material for the attacks by Assad supporters. One notorious

[39] Di Giovanni (2018).

[40] See DFRLab. (2018). "#BreakingSyria: Assad's search engine optimization". *Medium*. https://medium.com/dfrlab/breakingsyria-assads-search-engine-optimization-d16d7fc140f4.

[41] Freedland, J. (2018). "The great divide of our times is not left v right, but true v false". *The Guardian*. https://www.theguardian.com/commentisfree/2018/apr/20/trump-us-syria-truth-tribal-robert-mueller-white-helmets-factse.

example was the blunder of the so-called Mannequin Challenge, when some members of the group participated in the Internet craze in the hope of raising public awareness on their work, but it backfired as the images that were circulated stoked allegations about the staging of their rescues.[42] Critics of the White Helmets such as Vanessa Beeley as well as Russian Foreign Minister Lavrov seized on this opportunity and presented it as evidence that the group was using so-called crisis actors, another feature of conspiracy theorists' narratives. This claim was of course quickly debunked, but its on-line popularity resists to this day.[43]

4.5   Conclusions

The Syrian Civil War might be remembered as the first conflict in which the lines separating military and civilians, between material and narrative dimensions, and between facts and fictions became irreversibly blurred. As argued by Patrikarakos (2017), contemporary conflicts are characterized by a growing role of non-State actors and by a correlated surge in relevance of emotional and narrative dimensions. Non-State actors involved in contemporary conflicts know that they can attract international support if their pleas are heard by the global community. Activists, rebels and citizen journalists, who are at disadvantage from a military standpoint, attempt to win the conflict at the discursive level. The White Helmets' testimony of the civilian suffering is part of this strategy that characterized the discourse of the Syrian opposition since the early years of the uprising.

It is telling that the targeting of the White Helmets really started in the aftermath of the global wave of indignation that emerged after the search-and-rescue group posted the picture of Omran Daqneesh, a dazed boy four years old, covered in dust, who had been rescued when his house in East Aleppo was bombed in 2016. As the world wept for Omar, the Syrian regime and Russia swiftly pushed back by showing a completely

---

[42] Higgins, E. (2016). "There's no such thing as a good fake—When publicity stunts go wrong". *Bellingcat.* https://www.bellingcat.com/resources/articles/2016/11/30/theres-no-thing-good-fake-publicity-stunts-go-wrong/.

[43] Beeley, V. (2016). "WHITE HELMETS: The 'Mannequin Challenge', A publicity stunt that backfired? Vanessa Beeley talks to RT". *21st Century Wire.* https://21stcenturywire.com/2016/11/23/white-helmets-the-mannequin-challenge-a-publicity-stunt-that-backfired-vanessa-beeley-talks-to-rt/.

different set of pictures of him, clean and neatly groomed, accusing the White Helmets of manipulating the child against his parents' will.

Children's suffering put a human face to the thousands of nameless and faceless victims of the Syrian conflict and thus could move public opinions and governments to react. However, just as any YouTube video or tweet could become a piece of evidence about a suspected atrocity on the ground, it could as easily be refuted, decontextualized and challenged by an opposite narrative. This is the essential feature of post-truth condition that has plagued the Syria Civil War. The Syrian government and its ally Russia, with the amplification work of social media users, fought back against the opposition with effective counternarratives, by taking advantage of the constant flow of unfiltered and falsifiable information to confuse and distort the coverage of the events, and in some cases to spread outright falsehoods and disinformation.

The disinformation strategies employed in Syria are an example of Russian modern information warfare, aimed not exclusively at promoting a certain narrative, but also at confusing an issue with multiple narratives so that people can't recognize any truth (Pomerantsev and Weiss 2014). As discussed in Chapter 2, this has become a staple of Russian media manipulation strategies, both in domestic and in foreign politics. As former chess master and Russian activist Garry Kasparov tweeted in the aftermath of Trump election: "The point of modern propaganda isn't only to misinform or push an agenda. It is to exhaust your critical thinking, to annihilate truth."

The case study discussed in the previous sections illustrates how post-truth politics and communications operated in the context of conflict and foreign policy initiatives in the Middle East, particularly when resource-rich State actors such as Russia became involved in hybrid warfare campaigns to challenge the communications of non-State actors such as rebels and political oppositions. As seen, social media in the Arab Spring provided opportunities for citizens' expression and mobilization, but they were also co-opted as tools for government-sponsored propaganda and harassment of oppositional voices. What this research wished to emphasize is the tension between freedom and control, between liberation and repression that are visible around the political use of the Internet. In the intermediate space created by such tension is where post-truth in Syria flourished.

The social media war of narratives around the Syrian uprising can be seen to a certain extent as the very first historical antecedent to the post-truth crisis that later engulfed other parts of the world. The same independent journalism and UGC that initially empowered rebels were later exploited in disseminating a counternarrative that assisted the Syrian regime in crushing the resistance, regain most of its territory and, most of all, re-establish legitimacy in the eyes of the global community, mainly thanks to the Russian intervention in 2015. In the backdrop, there is the already mentioned crisis of authority of Western media and democratic institutions, which vast segments of the international public opinion considered complicit with a covert imperialistic effort to topple the Assad regime. To counter the uprising and its democratic narrative and to spread the anti-Western counternarrative of regime change and foreign plot, the Syrian regime decided to pursue a strategy of weaponization of the 'entropic' inclination of the new medium, fabricating and amplifying a plurality of narratives, spreading unsubstantiated rumors, blurring the lines between facts and fictions and exhausting any possible truth-seeking effort. If a pun can be allowed in this discussion of otherwise dramatic events, the Assad regime, assisted by Russia and by a global community of supporters, effectively established a 'regime of post-truth' (Harsin 2015) in Syria, with the goal of creating a self-serving informational chaos to be exploited for repressive political and military ends.

References

Atlantic Council. (2017). *Breaking Aleppo.* http://www.publications.atlanticcouncil.org/breakingaleppo/.

Czuperski, M., Herbst, J., Higgins, E., Hof, F., & Nimmo, B. (2016). *Distract, deceive, destroy: Putin at war in Syria.* Washington, DC: Atlantic Council.

Haddad, B. (2016). The debate over Syria has reached a dead end. *The Nation.* https://www.thenation.com/article/the-debate-over-syria-has-reached-a-dead-end/.

Harsin, J. (2015). Regimes of post truth, post politics, and attention economies. *Communication, Culture & Critique, 8*(2), 327–333.

Harsin, J. (2018). Post-truth and critical communication. *Oxford Research Encyclopedias.* https://doi.org/10.1093/acrefore/9780190228613.013.757.

Kalpokas, I. (2018). *A political theory of post-truth.* London: Palgrave Macmillan.

Lynch, M., Freelon, D., & Aday, S. (2014). *Blogs and bullets III: Syria's socially mediated civil war.* United States Institute of Peace. https://www.usip.org/publications/2014/01/syrias-socially-mediated-civil-war.

Patrikarakos, D. (2017). *War in 140 characters: How social media is reshaping conflict in the twenty-first century.* New York: Basic Books.

Pomerantsev, P., & Weiss, M. (2014). The menace of unreality: How the Kremlin weaponizes information, culture and money. *The Interpreter.* http://www.interpretermag.com/the-menace-of-unreality-how-the-kremlin-weaponizes-information-culture-and-money/.

Roudakova, N. (2017). *Losing Pravda: Ethics and the press in post-truth Russia.* Cambridge: Cambridge University Press.

Sienkiewicz, M. (2014). Start making sense: A three-tier approach to citizen journalism. *Media, Culture and Society, 36*(5), 691–701.

Singer, P., & Brooking, E. (2018). *LikeWar: The weaponization of social media.* Boston: Houghton Mifflin Harcourt.

The Syria Campaign. (2017). *Killing the truth.* https://thesyriacampaign.org/wp-content/uploads/2017/12/KillingtheTruth.pdf.

Trombetta, L. (2012, Spring/Summer). Altering courses in unknown waters: Interaction between traditional and new media during the first months of the Syrian uprising. *Global Media Journal* (German Edition), *2*(1): 1–6.

Trombetta, L. (2013). *Siria. Dagli Ottomani agli Asad. E oltre.* Milan: Mondadori.

Woolley, S., & Howard, P. (2018). *Computational propaganda.* Oxford: Oxford University Press.

CHAPTER 5

Tribal Politics: The Disruptive Effects of Social Media in the Global South

Abstract This chapter investigates the disruptive impact of social media in politically volatile contexts in the Global South. The controversial role of Facebook in facilitating hate speech and disinformation that led to widespread violence against the Rohingya Muslim minority in Myanmar will be discussed. The chapter will also analyze the role of Facebook subsidiary WhatsApp in allowing the circulation of disinformation during the 2018 general elections in Brazil, won by controversial far-right politician Jair Bolsonaro. The chapter discusses the problematic role of social media platforms as arbiters of global political speech, as their affordances and incentives tend to favor sensational and inflammatory content. The problem is compounded by the inability of State institutions, particularly in countries with a weak democratic tradition, to exert control and enforce oversight on the content of social media platforms.

Keywords Bolsonaro · WhatsApp · Brazil · Facebook · Myanmar · Hate speech

5.1   Introduction

This chapter looks at the disruptive political effects of social media platforms in the Global South, with a special focus on two case studies from Myanmar and Brazil. While the two countries present a different

G. Cosentino, *Social Media and the Post-Truth World Order*,
https://doi.org/10.1007/978-3-030-43005-4_5

socioeconomic profile, they share a common past of military rule—Brazil until 1985, Myanmar until 2010—followed by a transition to democracy. The Myanmar case study discusses the controversial role of Facebook in enabling on-line harassment campaigns that have led to widespread violence against the Rohingya Muslim minority by the Myanmar army and by Buddhist extremists. The case study discusses how the Facebook affordances and incentives, as well its Free Basics initiative, played a role in spreading disinformation and hate speech in Myanmar, a country lacking a pluralistic media system and a robust tradition of journalism (Vaidhyanathan 2018). The second case study looks at the influence of WhatsApp, a subsidiary of Facebook, in spreading disinformation during the 2018 presidential elections that brought to power Jair Bolsonaro, a far-right army veteran, who rose to prominence thanks to his penchant for controversy and his radically conservative stance on several political issues, from LGBTQ rights to police brutality.

In both cases studies, weak or fragilized democratic institutions and the emergence of a social media-centered information ecosystem are discussed as correlated preconditions for the rise of far-right nationalistic movements. The profit-maximizing tendency of global technology companies, and their inability and reluctance to self-regulate and accept stricter government oversight, compounded the problem under observation. The tendency of social media platform to enable ideological echo chambers is linked to the 'tribalization' of public opinion that can escalate in interethnic and political harassment and violence, especially in countries where family networks and clans play an important political role.

5.2   Fanning the Flames of Hate: The Role of Facebook in the Rohingya Genocide

In August 2017, militants from the armed group Arakan Rohingya Salvation Army attacked a number of police and military posts in the Rakhine State in northwestern Myanmar, at the border with Bangladesh. The attack came after a surge in sectarian tensions between the Buddhist majority and the Rohingya Muslim minority. The Rohingyas are a stateless minority that has suffered decades of oppression and persecution sanctioned by the Myanmar government, including the denial of citizenship rights.[1] The decades-old strife between Muslims and Buddhists in Myanmar, which is also linked to the complex legacy of the British colonial presence (George and Venkiteswaran 2019), escalated since the country started its democratic transition in 2012, following decades of military rule.

The retaliation against the Muslim militants by the Myanmar army, also known as Tatmadaw, was brutal and widespread. According to official accounts by the United Nations,[2] grave crimes against humanity such as ethnic cleansing were committed by the Myanmar military, assisted by armed extremists from the Buddhist majority, as they attacked Rohingya villages, burned homes, beat and killed people, including children and infants, raped women and girls and forced hundreds of thousands to flee their homes. Buddhist citizens were also attacked by Muslim armed groups, but the Rohingya minority overwhelmingly bore the brunt of the violent exacerbation of the ethnic tensions. While reports vary, the military backlash against the Rohingyas is said to have caused the death of nearly ten thousand people and the massive exodus of nearly seven hundred thousand into Bangladesh and other neighboring countries.

The UN accounts of the conflict were widely covered by broadcast media and discussed on social media, but they were rejected by the Myanmar government, which also initially refused to issue visas for a UN fact-finding mission to the Rakhine State. After the first rumors and reports documenting the violent repression against the Rohingya started to circulate on-line, Myanmar's de facto leader and Nobel laureate Aung San Suu Kyi dismissed the claims that crimes amounting to genocide had been committed by the army. Faced with mounting international pressure, Aung San Suu Kyi also resorted to what has become a trope in today's Internet-driven political communications, pioneered by Donald Trump, which is the use of the term 'fake news' to dismiss criticism. Attracting widespread condemnation,

---

[1] "Since the 1970s, successive Burmese governments have sought to reduce the Muslim population in parts of Rakhine State by not issuing them new citizenship cards, and restricting their access to healthcare, educational institutions, and economic opportunities, among other means" (Fink 2018).

[2] United Nations Human Rights Office of the High Commissioner. (2018). *Myanmar: UN Fact-Finding Mission releases its full account of massive violations by military in Rakhine, Kachin and Shan States.* https://www.ohchr.org/EN/NewsEvents/Pages/DisplayNews.aspx?NewsID=23575&LangID=E.

Aung San Suu Kyi labeled the reports a 'huge iceberg of misinformation'[3] that was distorting the public perception of what was happening in the Rakhine State. She also said that fake news and disinformation were igniting the tensions in the region to the advantage of
Muslim terrorists. The exacerbation of the tensions in Rakhine led to a
worldwide demonstration of support for the Rohingyas, especially from
Muslim countries, that generated over one million tweets and several
trending hashtags.[4]

The surge in violence in the Rakhine State was accompanied by a war of
narratives on the events on ground, similar to that seen in the Syrian Civil
War. As observed by Kayleigh Long, a journalist with extensive experience
in Myanmar, "for every conflict that plays out on the ground in Myanmar
today, there's a parallel one being waged in cyberspace, by activists, ethnic
armed groups, political parties, civilian government actors, and the army
itself."[5] Such conflict was characterized by what Jonathan Head of the
BBC called a "slew of misleading images being shared on social media,"
especially Facebook, consisting of inflammatory audio-visual documentation, a good part of it patently false.[6]

The problem of disinformation via social media in the Rohingya crisis
was compounded by the absence of a free and independent press, another
parallelism with the phenomenon discussed in the previous chapter. After
2012, as Myanmar experienced a rapid transition from a military rule to
a democracy, the country couldn't develop "a mature and professional
media system or a tradition of professional journalism" (Vaidhyanathan
2018, 688) that could provide objective and reliable coverage of domestic
politics. Also, just as in Syria the Assad regime prevented foreign press to
access combat zones, creating opportunities for one-sided reporting and
propaganda, disinformation in the Rohingya crisis emerged because the

---

[3] BBC News. (2017). "Rohingya crisis: Suu Kyi says fake news helping terrorists". *BBC News.* https://www.bbc.com/news/world-asia-41170570.

[4] Rannard, G. (2017). "Rohingya crisis: What's behind these 1.2 million tweets?" *BBC News.* https://www.bbc.com/news/blogs-trending-41160953.

[5] Long, K. (2019). "The war for truth in Myanmar's cyberspace". *Coda.* https://codastory.com/authoritarian-tech/myanmar-facebook-conflict-rakhine/.

[6] As an example, a widely circulating picture supposedly showing Rohingya militants was in fact a photograph of Bangladeshi fighting in the 1971 independence war. See Head, J. (2017). "Myanmar conflict fake photos inflame tension". *BBC.* https://www.bbc.com/news/world-asia-41123878.

Myanmar government didn't allow journalists, the United Nations missions or human rights bodies to access the areas interested by the interethnic conflict. Disinformation and misinformation then occurred when war coverage was infused with propaganda efforts, both by the governments and by insurgents, and in the absence of external, trusted independent bodies that could verify what was being circulated. The result was that the international public opinion relied on conflicting accounts on the Rohingya crisis that were then received through preexisting ideological prisms and cognitive biases, allowing for distortions and manipulations. The conflict of narratives around the events in Rakhine continued well after the forced displacement of thousands of Rohingya. In 2018, the Myanmar Army Department of Public Relations and Psychological Warfare sponsored the publication of a book,[7] containing several inaccurate information, aimed at rewriting the historical background to the violent events in Rakhine. The book implied that the Rohingyas were immigrants from Bangladesh intent on carving a separate Muslim state in the northwestern region, a notion that that is contested by the Muslim minority and that echoes the Chinese justification for repressing the Uighur minority in the Xinjiang region.

The crisis in Myanmar is regarded by many as a striking example of the dangerous impact of social media, especially Facebook, in both enabling disinformation and exacerbating sectarian strife in politically volatile countries characterized by frail democratic institutions. The political impact of Facebook in Myanmar is linked to the peculiar conditions of technological development of the telecommunications sector in a country that experienced dramatic transformations in the transition from military rule to democracy. Because the junta that had ruled the country had kept its citizens controlled and isolated for several decades, up until 2012 only 1% of the total Myanmar population used the Internet. In 2013, a democratically elected quasi-civil government oversaw the deregulation of the telecommunication sector, with the state-owned phone company facing competition from two foreign mobile phone companies. As a result, the country experienced what has been called the "fastest digital rollout in

---

[7] On top of several inaccurate historical claims, the book also included several fake photographic documents, according to a Reuters report published by *The Guardian*. See *The Guardian*. (2018). "Myanmar army fakes photos and history in sinister rewrite of Rohingya crisis". *The Guardian*. https://www.theguardian.com/world/2018/aug/31/myanmar-army-fakes-photos-and-history-in-sinister-rewrite-of-rohingya-crisis.

human history"[8]: prices of SIM cards dropped from $200 to $2, and by 2016, nearly half the population had mobile phone subscriptions with Internet access. In this booming market of mobile connectivity, the Facebook app became immediately very popular, as it offered a messaging system, news and entertainment in a single package. To further entice customers, mobile phone operators began offering the use of Facebook without data charges, making the use of the app even more widespread. As a result, the number of Facebook users grew rapidly, and it stands currently at roughly 25 million, in a country of about 50 million people.

In August 2013, Facebook CEO Mark Zuckerberg announced a plan to make the Internet available for the first time to billions of people in developing countries, an initiative which goes under the label of Internet.org. Part of Internet.org is Free Basics, an app "that offers users in developing markets a 'free' Facebook-centric version of the broader internet. (…) The app provides users willing to sign up for Facebook with internet access that doesn't count against their mobile plan."[9] While presented as an ambitious humanitarian initiative aimed at providing Internet access to people in the world who couldn't afford it, Free Basics was also part of Facebook's expansionistic strategy in the Global South, a potentially enormous market for its financial future. By subsidizing access to Facebook via mobile phones, Free Basics further popularized the use of Facebook in Myanmar,[10] reinforcing the perception in the country that there was no distinction between the social media platform and the broader Internet.[11]

Facebook has had a transformative effect on people's lives in Myanmar, mostly for the good, "providing them with newfound freedom to obtain information, express themselves, and connect with others" (Fink 2018). However, the sudden popularization of Facebook in a country that didn't

---

[8] Long (2019).

[9] Hatmaker, T. (2018). "Facebook Free Basic program ended quietly in Myanmar". *TechCrunch*. https://techcrunch.com/2018/05/01/facebook-free-basics-ending-myanmar-internet-org/.

[10] The service was discontinued after September 2017, officially as part of a regulatory effort by the Myanmar government.

[11] "Telecommunications data indicates Facebook accounted for as much as 80 percent of daily in-country web traffic at its peak, with most browsing of external sites taking place through the platform" (Long 2019).

have a robust media system and a tradition of journalism caused for sig-nification distortion in the process of information production and circu-lation. For many, Facebook was the main gateway to access information and to connect with relatives and friends.[12] Rumors circulating among family or friends' networks on Facebook were perceived as indistinguish-able from verified news by its users. As observed by Vaidhyanathan, under the Myanmar military rule, "rumor was the dominant form of 'news' and the chief subject of discussion. So, through Facebook, old habits thrive" (Vaidhyanathan 2018, 689). Since other reputable sources of informa-tion are almost nonexistent in the country, unverified information and emotionally charged rumors run rampant on the social media platform, and when "shared among trusted friends and family members, they can become conventional wisdom."[13]

At the beginning of Myanmar's democratic transition, a Buddhist ultra-nationalist movement emerged, empowered by the government support of nationalist sentiments and also fueled by the anxieties associated with the broader political transformations underway in the country. In the fol-lowing years, such movement has made an "effective use of Facebook to create a virtual community linked by shared fears" (Fink 2018) associated with the presence of Muslims across the country, and especially with the Rohingya population concentrated in parts of the Rakhine State. Both on-line and off-line Buddhist ultranationalists, including prominent monks who enjoy high moral authority among the population, have criticized Muslims for presenting a threat to the largely Buddhist nation, pointing to "high Muslim birthrates, increasing Muslim economic influence, and Muslim plans to take over the country" (Fink 2018).

Nationalist ideologies, however different in their origin and goals, often coalesce around the same grievances and common enemies. The Islamophobic rhetoric of Myanmar Buddhists presents many parallels with the anti-immigration discourse espoused by White nationalists in Western

---

[12] This phenomenon is not limited to Myanmar, but it is common to other developing countries. See Mirani, L. (2015). "Millions of Facebook users have no idea they're using the internet". *Quartz.* https://qz.com/333313/milliions-of-facebook-users-have-no-idea-theyre-using-the-internet/.

[13] Taub, A., & Fisher, M. (2018). "Where countries are Tinderboxes and Facebook is a match". *The New York Times.* https://www.nytimes.com/2018/04/21/world/asia/facebook-sri-lanka-riots.html.

countries discussed in Chapter 3. Around 2014, Buddhist ultranationalists started spreading rumors on Facebook of a "global Muslim conspiracy bent on ridding the world of Buddhism. Through Facebook they have called for boycotts of Muslim-owned businesses, a ban on interfaith marriages, and limitations on rights for Muslims who live in Myanmar" (Vaidhyanathan 2018, 689). In July of 2014, anti-Muslim riots broke out in Mandalay after false rumors spread, shared on Facebook by the prominent Buddhist monk Wirathu, alleging the rape of a Buddhist woman by a Muslim man.[14] Wirathu essentially acted as a nationalist political influencer, in the same vein as alt-right personalities or pro-Assad Twitter stars have done in different contexts, signaling the key role played by opinion leaders in shaping social media conversations and in amplifying disinformation.

Facebook also offered a powerful platform for the propaganda efforts of the Myanmar government and army. In the new age of widespread connectivity, the Myanmar authorities could not resort to the censorship of the Internet and the press as they had done in the years prior to the democratic transition. They resorted instead to employ disinformation as a strategy for controlling and manipulating the public opinion, a tendency common to other countries with autocratic tendencies, as we have seen in the chapters dedicated to Russia and Syria. As observed by an independent analyst working on Myanmar: "Crushing censorship was rapidly replaced with a cacophony of social media, where agitprop could hide better and be more effectively insidious."[15] Also, as seen in other examples of computational propaganda, from Pizzagate to the disinformation campaign against the White Helmets, the combination of sock-puppet accounts and political bots was often used also in Myanmar to create the perception of either popular support or widespread opposition to a political idea.

Facebook had thus a major role in circulating false information and hate speech against the Rohingyas and other Muslim minorities in Myanmar. The UN fact-finding mission declared that inflammatory content circulating on the platform had a 'determining role' in igniting hatred. As reported by a United Nations investigator: "Facebook was used to incite

---

[14] Stecklow, S. (2018). "Why Facebook is losing the war on hate speech in Myanmar". *Reuters.* https://www.reuters.com/investigates/special-report/myanmar-facebook-hate/.

[15] Long (2019).

violence and hatred against the Muslim minority group" through thousands of "posts, comments, images and videos attacking the Rohingya or other Myanmar Muslims."[16] Buddhist ultranationalists have taken advantage of Facebook, its popularity and its ease of access "to stoke fear, normalize hateful views, and facilitate acts of violence against Muslims in Myanmar" (Fink 2018).

The Myanmar example mirrors several other examples from countries such as Sri Lanka and Indonesia, where Facebook played a significant role in stoking deeply rooted ethnic tension. *The New York Times* collected several case studies from Southeast Asia that demonstrate how the social media platform was instrumental in exacerbating local ethnic strife. Yet, as the journalistic investigation suggests, the company response was insufficient in curbing the problem. The interethnic problems predated the arrival of Facebook, of course, but its aggressive marketing and unsupervised popularization produced a quick exacerbation of existing political issues. As *The New York Times* reporters conclude, "Facebook did not create (...) anti-Rohingya sentiment in Myanmar. But the platform, by supercharging content that taps into tribal identity, can upset fragile communal balances."[17]

This tendency is strictly linked to the rewarding mechanisms inscribed in the Facebook algorithm that tends to prioritize content that keeps users engaged, regardless of its veracity or its potential to incite controversies. As also observed in the United States and Europe, the dynamics of engagement on Facebook are often correlated with the spread of misinformation and hate speech (Silverman et al. 2016; Vaidhyanathan 2018). The Facebook interface rewards "engagement, delivering a dopamine boost when users accrue likes and responses, training users to indulge behaviors that win affirmation. And because its algorithm unintentionally privileges negativity, the greatest rush comes by attacking outsiders: The other sports team. The other political party. The ethnic minority."[18] Such tendency reinforces another detrimental effect of social media such as the phenomenon of political polarization. However, while in the West political polarization driven by social media often takes the form of ideological bickering and, in the worst-case scenarios, of radicalization of terrorist

---

[16] Stecklow (2018).

[17] Taub and Fisher (2018).

[18] Ibid.

groups, in the Global South, the phenomenon of polarization has led to the re-emergence of tribal politics. Facebook's most dangerous impact in the Global South is thus the amplification of a tendency toward the tribalization of the public opinion, which has in turn sparked riots, lynching and violent actions by improvised vigilantes.

As the Facebook Newsfeed in Myanmar became the primary access point to news, in the process displacing local media as information outlets, the local government could not enforce oversight on the type of content that was circulated, nor exert effective leverage on the company to take countermeasures against disinformation and hate speech. As it has happened with the real-life actions by White ethnonationalists and conspiracy theorists that were radicalized on-line, hate speech and disinformation via Facebook fomented real-world attacks, both in Myanmar and in other Southeast Asian countries.

This dangerous tendency, already presented before the 2017 escalation of Rohingya persecution, was compounded by the ineffective response by Facebook to tackle the problem. The company devoted very few resources to curb hate speech in Myanmar, and for years, it ignored several warnings on its potential violent escalation, resisting pressure to hire moderators. While researchers, NGOs and human rights activists had warned Facebook prior to the 2017 conflict that its platform was being used to stir tensions and to ignite hatred against the Muslims, in particular the Rohingya, Facebook didn't sufficiently address such alerts. As with other countries in the Global South, the more critical issue was the insufficient moderation of the platform. In early 2015, well after the first resurfacing of the ethnic strife between Buddhists and Muslims, there were only two people at Facebook who could speak Burmese in charge of reviewing problematic posts. Before that, "most of the people reviewing Burmese content spoke English,"[19] and thus couldn't effectively monitor and control the use of slurs, derogatory terms and inflammatory language.

In a belated attempt to address its past inertia, Facebook announced its intention to improve its moderating efforts in Myanmar by hiring a hundred native Burmese speakers to review content on the platform. According to researcher Christina Fink, "This is critical, because a largely technological approach, focused primarily on artificial intelligence searches for key words, is too crude" (Fink 2018). As a result, in 2018, the company

[19] Stecklow (2018).

acted on over fifty thousand pieces of content for violating its hate speech policies. Facebook also banned accounts and pages associated with Myanmar military personnel that were indicated by the UN as being directedly responsible for the ethnic cleansing in Rakhine.[20] The banned accounts had a widespread reach in the country, as they were followed by nearly 12 million accounts, which is about half of all Myanmar's Facebook users.

The actions toward more attentive moderation and policing of hate speech by Facebook are as belated as they are welcome. Executives at the social media platform are finally realizing that the tools they have created allow nationalist movements to manipulate citizens with disinformation, stir violent sentiments against minorities and mobilize them toward violence and harassment campaign. Interethnic tensions and nationalistic tendencies have always existed, but they couldn't rely on a platform that rewards and amplifies negative emotions and inflammatory content as quickly and as widely as Facebook. As observed by Vaidhyanathan, "Facebook does not favor hatred. But hatred favors Facebook" (Vaidhyanathan 2018, 692).

5.3 How WhatsApp Brought Bolsonaro to Power in Brazil

While Facebook and Twitter are the most popular social media platforms for accessing information and engaging with political content in most parts of the world, in some countries of the Global South the messaging app WhatsApp, a subsidiary of Facebook, is the most prominent outlet of political communication. According to a Tactical Tech report, "WhatsApp is increasingly becoming the main tool for political campaigns in the Global South, and its influence is continuing to grow."[21]

WhatsApp has specific features that make it an effective outlet of political communication and campaigning, especially in parts of the world where Internet coverage is poor or inconsistent. The messaging platform—allowing one-to-one communication as well as group communication up to 256 people—enjoys high penetration particularly in rural communities where Internet access occurs primarily via smartphones. The

[20] Ibid.

[21] Rennó, R., et al. (2018). "WhatsApp: The widespread use of WhatsApp in political campaigning in the Global South". *Tactical Tech.* https://ourdataourselves.tacticaltech. org/posts/whatsapp/.

relatively large size of its groups allows to create communities of familiar people, with messages coming often from contacts known to the user, thus adding a feeling of intimacy and reliability to the communications. This feature represents a strong factor in traditional communities where politics is often intertwined with family or tribal affiliations. Also, political content on WhatsApp can circulate quickly and widely due to the speed of the message delivery that "can create a feeling of urgency about particular topics."[22] Starting from 2016, WhatsApp also enabled end-to-end encryption to the communications via the platform, allowing a high level of security and privacy. Politicians, activists and campaigners in world regions where the penetration of traditional media and the Internet is still low, or where there is a threat of political persecution, can thus rely on a fast, effective and secure communication system that allows them to inform citizens about party activities, to shape and influence political discourse, to create a direct connection with their constituencies and to mobilize voters.

However, just as with other social media, the use of WhatsApp for political ends has been tainted by disinformation, hate speech and defamatory messages. Insular communities on social media have proven fertile grounds of misinformation and political polarization, particularly in the context of weak or fragilized democratic contexts lacking an independent media system and a tradition of professional journalism, as seen in the previous sections. These structural problems are exacerbated by the fact that in some parts of the world Internet access is still unreliable, thus limiting the ability of users to fact-check the information that is sent through WhatsApp.

In countries with uneven Internet coverage, this problem is compounded by the practice known as 'zero rating,' by which telecommunication companies offer free data to mobile phone users for the exclusive use of Facebook or WhatsApp, as observed also in the case of Myanmar. While convenient for customers, the practice has the same problems encountered by the Free Basics Facebook initiative, as it discourages users from visiting other web sites or other social media platforms, and it hinders the possibility of fact-checking. As observed by the Tactical Tech reports, citizens often receive via WhatsApp political messages that are either decontextualized or carry few links to more information. In both

---

[22] Ibid.

cases, users often don't have access to the Internet to verify the messages received.

With around 120 million users out of a total population of 209 million, WhatsApp is one of the main sources of information in Brazil, and it plays a major role in its politics. Because of the zero rating offer, WhatsApp has in some ways taken the role that Facebook or Twitter plays in other countries. Brazilians who cannot afford an Internet plan can still use WhatsApp unlimitedly, as many mobile phone operators allow free WhatsApp access to their subscribers. As a result, many people in Brazil use the messaging app to receive information on a plurality of subjects, including politics. Among Brazilian WhatsApp users, nearly 50% of them receive political or electoral information via the platform.[23] During the electoral campaign leading up to the 2018 general elections, won by controversial far-right candidate Jair Bolsonaro against center-left candidate Fernando Haddad, WhatsApp was arguably the most prominent medium of political communication, as well as the channel for the most conspicuous circulation of disinformation.

WhatsApp was preferred over traditional media by some candidates, including Bolsonaro, because the Brazilian electoral law didn't regulate it as stringently as other communication channels, in terms of both distribution of electoral messages via the platform and for their content. In 2018, several marketing agencies in Brazil offered electoral campaigning services targeted for WhatsApp. These agencies collected citizens' contact information through a plurality of legal and illegal ways, often by scraping thousands of Facebook profiles,[24] which allowed them to assemble vast list of users who were targeted with frequent messages.[25] The content of those messages was often problematic, including misinformation, misleading statement, slandering and harassment of political opponents.

[23] Tardáguila, C., et al. (2018). "Fake news is poisoning Brazilian politics. WhatsApp can stop it". *The New York Times*. https://www.nytimes.com/2018/10/17/opinion/brazil-election-fake-news-whatsapp.html.

[24] Magenta, M., et al. (2018). "How WhatsApp is being abused in Brazil's elections". *BBC News*. https://www.bbc.com/news/technology-45956557.

[25] Rennó, R., et al. (2018). See also Tactical Tech. (2018). "Brazilian elections and the public-private data trade". https://ourdataourselves.tacticaltech.org/posts/overview-brazil/.

As highlighted by the Coding Rights report *Data and Elections in Brazil 2018* "The lack of provisions in the electoral reform regarding content shared on WhatsApp and the intricacies of the platform have made it almost impossible for electoral content to be flagged or even to assure candidates that it will not be used for illicit purposes, such as online political advertising outside the authorized or propagation of hate speech or the so-called fake news" (Coding Rights 2018, 75). According to the authors of a report on disinformation during the 2018 general elections in Brazil, in a sample of over a hundred thousand political images shared via WhatsApp, "56 percent of the most-shared images were misleading. Only 8 percent of the 50 most widely shared images were considered fully truthful."[26]

The report also highlights the dynamics and tactics of the spreading of disinformation via WhatsApp, suggesting that politicians and their supporters "rely on a combined pyramid and network strategy in which producers create malicious content and broadcast it to regional and local activists, who then spread the messages widely to public and private groups. From there, the messages travel even further as they are forwarded on by believing individuals to their own contacts."[27] The social dynamics of family networks and clans, combined with top-down propaganda strategies, thus played a key role in propagating misleading or harmful content via WhatsApp.

An anti-establishment candidate with a penchant for provocative statements such as Bolsonaro found in WhatsApp an ideal communication environment, as it better suited his maverick style of campaigning. Apparently without relying on political marketing professionals, Bolsonaro made WhatsApp the core of his campaigning in 2018, managing personally his account and preparing content for frequent communication and exchanges with his supporters. Through a wide number of WhatsApp groups, Bolsonaro supporters actively shared via the platform—and through an ecosystem of far-right web sites and social media

[26] One of the most famous examples of false images was a picture purporting to show a young Dilma Rousseff, the former president of Brazil impeached in 2016, next to Fidel Castro, suggesting that she had had been his student. Mrs. Rousseff was not, however, the woman of the picture. Still, as noted by Tardáguila et al. (2018) "such images are effective in smearing Ms. Rousseff and the Workers' Party — of which Mr. Haddad is a member — in a country where there is much antipathy to communism among the middle class".

[27] Ibid.

pages—the messages of their candidate, much more actively than other candidates' supporters.[28] These groups have often acted as breeding ground for disinformation, on-line lynching and harassment campaigns, as well as for the spreading of far-right politics, with some groups acting "as incubators for pro-gun, pro-torture, and anti-abortion memes."[29]

The Bolsonaro campaign has been heavily criticized for relying on disinformation, and it has also been accused of electoral fraud. According to an investigation by one of the major newspapers in the country, the *Folha de São Paulo*, Bolsonaro had received illegal donation by a group of Brazilian entrepreneurs in order to fund a million-dollar disinformation campaign against Haddad via WhatsApp.[30] As a result, WhatsApp banned around 100,000 accounts used to spread fake news, including the account of Bolsonaro's son. In some cases, international SIM cards were used to bypass WhatsApp spam controls. It should be pointed out that Bolsonaro's campaign wasn't the only one trafficking in disinformation in 2018, as the PT party[31] and its supporters also resorted to attacking its main rival through false information.[32]

The 2018 elections occurred in a typical post-truth context characterized by a trust crisis suffered by public institutions and by heightened political polarization (Machado et al. 2018), partly due to a widespread corruption scandal—the so-called Operation Car Wash—that in the years prior had rocked the Brazilian political establishment, particularly politicians of the left-wing PT party, and led to the impeachment of former Prime Minister Dilma Rousseff and the contested incarceration of two-time Prime Minister Lula. Such polarized context, where a cynical and

---

[28] Rennó et al. (2018).

[29] Rocha, Y. (2018). "How Brazil's Trump is using WhatsApp to win election". *Fast Company*. https://www.fastcompany.com/90256810/how-brazils-trump-is-using-whatsapp-to-win-election.

[30] Phillips, D. (2018a). "Bolsonaro business backers accused of illegal WhatsApp fake news campaign". *The Guardian*. https://www.theguardian.com/world/2018/oct/18/brazil-jair-bolsonaro-whatsapp-fake-news-campaign.

[31] PT stands for 'Partido dos Trabalhadores' (Workers' Party).

[32] Bolsonaro was accused of wanting to increase taxes on the poorest, and fake stories started spreading after a knife attack that left Bolsonaro seriously injured one month before the elections, alleging that it had been staged to boost his popularity. See Phillips, D. (2018b). "Brazil battles fake news 'tsunami' amid polarized presidential election". *The Guardian*. https://www.theguardian.com/world/2018/oct/18/brazil-jair-bolsonaro-whatsapp-fake-news-campaign.

disaffected public opinion resorted to alternative channels of communication and welcomed anti-establishment candidates and discourses, enabled the rise of radical politicians relying on sensational or false information. This scenario bears many similarities with the conditions that paved the way for the Trump presidency in the United States, or for the Brexit referendum, and in general for the wave of populist and right-wing movements that have surged in several liberal democracies around the world.

While Facebook and Twitter were also involved in the spread of fake news during the 2018 general elections,[33] the prominence of a WhatsApp as a platform for political messages among Brazilians led to many false or misleading textual messages, pictures or memes to spread via the messaging app. Also, as Facebook was more closely scrutinized by various fact-checking initiatives, disinformation tactics were pushed to WhatsApp, where they couldn't be as easily monitored.[34] Facebook and Google have collaborated on an initiative called Comprova, which brought together a consortium of Brazilian news organization that joined forces to fact-check tips about suspicious information and debunk fake or misleading content.[35] Comprova also discovered various videos on WhatsApp that were either fake or presented out of context.[36] However, as reported by *The New York Times*, "many Brazilians view the work of the fact-checkers as part of a nefarious effort by big corporations like Facebook to shield Brazilians from the truth," which is an another indication that the 2018 general election occurred in the deeply fractured and suspicious information environment, where no trusted institution could be granted truth-arbitering authority (Harsin 2018). This also explains why WhatsApp, an information environment whose messages couldn't be effectively scrutinized for their veracity by public or private institutions,

---

[33] Phillips (2018b).

[34] Tardáguila et al. (2018).

[35] Ibid.

[36] "One clip purporting to show leftwing supporters attacking a car with a Bolsonaro sticker was found to be from a 2017 protest against the current president Michel Temer. A viral image showing the leftwing VP candidate Manuela D'Avila with tattoos of Vladimir Lenin and Che Guevara was quickly found to be false". See Kaiser, A. J. (2018). "The Brazilian group scanning WhatsApp for in run-up to elections". *The Guardian.* https://www.theguardian.com/world/2018/sep/26/brazil-elections-comprova-project-misiniformation-whatsapp.

became so popular among ruthless campaigners as well as among a highly polarized and volatile Brazilian electorate.

The popularity of the platform as a tool for family members to connect among themselves also facilitated the spread of false information, with family groups being responsible for 51% of disinformation on WhatsApp, according to research conducted at the University of Sao Paulo.[37] As seen also in the example of political rumors that spread through family networks in Myanmar, the dynamics of large family or friends' groups were important factors in enabling disinformation via WhatsApp. Also, sensational or slandering information could be shared in the relative safety of a familiar group, without the risk of attracting the public criticism or shaming that occurs in open platforms like Facebook and Twitter.[38] Families and family values were also important themes of political discussion, as most of the disinformation circulating during the two rounds of the general election was stemming out a culture war on LGBTQ rights, specifically the sexual education of children on homosexuality and homophobia.

One of the main topics of the Bolsonaro campaign was its staunch opposition to an educational program of Haddad's party aiming at fighting homophobia among Brazilian children and teens. The attack line of Bolsonaro, around which myriads of memes and fake news were produced and distributed via social media, primarily via WhatsApp, was that the PT candidates wanted to 'sexualise' children and entice them toward homosexuality via the distribution of a so-called gay kit. Bolsonaro, a self-declared and unabashed homophobe,[39] has been railing against the existence of an alleged conspiracy by progressive academics and teachers to 'pervert' children since 2012,[40] a topic that has resonated well with many Brazilian families that in large numbers still consider sexual education of

[37] Rennó et al. (2018).

[38] Long, C. (2018). "Why WhatsApp is Brazil's go-to political weapon". *The Brazilian Report.* https://brazilian.report/society/2018/04/13/whatsapp-fake-news-elections/.

[39] Amis, L., & Fiori, J. (2018). "The torturer". *The Los Angeles Review of Books.* https://lareviewofbooks.org/article/the-torturer/?fbclid= IwAR12RgOZu0UM4OjCpd3llgraVVDvSwsODW98OLXaxNtj2C6eW7Cs9wgKrrU.

[40] Fisher, M., & Taub, A. (2019). "How YouTube radicalized Brazil". *The New York Times.* https://www.nytimes.com/2019/08/11/world/americas/youtube-brazil.html.

children to be the exclusive responsibility of their parents.[41] Such conspiratorial thinking again reflects the White nationalists' anxieties about a feminist or LGBTQ plot aimed at the emasculation of Western men, a frequent theme in the alt-right manosphere (Marwick and Lewis 2017).

While the encryption embedded in the platform makes it virtually impossible to estimate the number of people in Brazil exposed to false information via WhatsApp, Brazilian fact-checkers that have worked on the most popular examples of fake news making the rounds in the 2018 campaign estimate that tens of millions of citizens might have been reached.[42]

Facebook became aware earlier during the 2018 electoral cycle of the misuse of WhatsApp as a channel for disinformation in Brazil. The main problem faced by Facebook in addressing the issue of disinformation via WhatsApp has been the difficulty in creating a balance between allowing people to have private and safe conversation on the one hand, and stopping the spread of false information on the other.[43] The company has no control over the encrypted communication, and it can't enforce the removal of a flagged content as they can do on their parent social media platform Facebook, or as Twitter can. Facebook did, however, implement some measures to stop the spreading of malicious contentment via WhatsApp: group admins were given more control over users' ability to send messages, and forwarded messages were flagged to distinguish them from original messages.

Nonetheless, these measures were deemed insufficient by the same group of scholars and journalists[44] that issued the already mentioned disinformation report on the 2018 general elections in Brazil. Right before the elections, the group wrote a piece on *The New York Times* advocating

---

[41] Cotroneo, R. (2018). "Brasile, allarme fake news su WhatsApp alle presidenziali. Il Tribunale elettorale: «Ci vogliono misure severe»". *Corriere della Sera*. https://www.corriere.it/tecnologia/18_ottobre_16/brasile-allarme-fake-news-whatsapp-presidenziali-tribunale-elettorale-ci-vogliono-misure-severe-2b012770-d158-11e8-81a5-27b20bf95b8c.shtml.

[42] Ibid.

[43] Daniels, C. (2018). "How WhatsApp is fighting misinformation in Brazil". *Facebook*. https://about.fb.com/news/h/how-whatsapp-is-fighting-misinformation-in-brazil/.

[44] Tardáguila et al. (2018).

for stricter measures to be taken by WhatsApp immediately before elections, in order to limit the detrimental effects of disinformation. In particular, the researchers suggested that WhatsApp should have restricted the number of times that a message could be forwarded from twenty to five. As part of a broader effort to curb disinformation, WhatsApp had previously reduced the number of messages that can be forwarded from 256 to 20. In India, however, where WhatsApp was implicated with cases of lynching, the limit is five.[45] The restriction of broadcasts, meaning the number of contacts to which a single user to send a message, was also requested, together with the limit to the size of new groups. WhatsApp responded to these requests by saying that there wasn't enough time to implement the changes before the elections, a notion that was, however, disputed by the Brazilians researchers.[46]

5.4   Conclusions

The case studies presented in this chapter are examples of how social media platforms have enabled disinformation and hate speech in weak or fragile democracies with a past of authoritarian politics and military rule. In both cases, politicians and authorities either exploited or failed to control the disruptive effects of new media platforms, hindering a constructive public dialogue respectful of minorities that could ensure a safe transition or continuation of democratic politics. In the Myanmar example, the fast emergence of a Facebook-centric information system to the detriment of a pluralistic and accountable press facilitated the spread of rumors and false narratives targeting Muslim minorities. In Brazil, a general climate of distrust toward the political establishment created the conditions for radical conservative politics to emerge via social media platforms such as WhatsApp, championing a discriminating agenda against LGBTQ and progressive politics.

While the evidence and the examples provided point to the undeniable responsibility of technology companies such as Facebook in facilitating the spread of disinformation and hate speech in the two countries

---

[45] Goel, V., et al. (2018). "How WhatsApp leads mobs to murder in India". *The New York Times.* https://www.nytimes.com/interactive/2018/07/18/technology/whatsapp-india-killings.html.

[46] Tardáguila et al. (2018).

under examination, the historical and political contexts of both countries should caution against a strictly technological deterministic reading of the phenomenon. The comparative dimension of this work should help locating the examples in a broader theoretical and historical framework, which takes into account social, economic and political considerations. The attacks against Muslims by Buddhist ultranationalists, while rooted in the specific history of Myanmar, have become exacerbated alongside a global wave of Islamophobia in multiple countries, as discussed in Chapter 3, which is linked also to the rise of Islamic fundamentalism, to the emergence of xenophobic sentiments around the world and which has also sparked violent reactions by White ethnonationalists in the West. Therefore, the role of social media platform in promoting hate speech, such as the anti-Rohingya movement in Myanmar, needs to be placed in the context of the global spread of radical, nationalist movements, who often target minorities, and of the failure of democratic institutions to protect multiculturalism and diversity. As for the example of Brazil, WhatsApp magnified tendencies of political radicalization that preexisted the advent of the platform. These considerations, however, don't exempt global technology companies from their responsibility in allowing hateful, defamatory or misleading content to run rampant on their platforms, especially in light of the fact that repeated warnings were given by scholars and civil society actors about the critical impact of social media in politically volatile contexts.

REFERENCES

Coding Rights. (2018). *Analysis of the playing field for the influence industry in preparation for the Brazilian general elections.* https://www.codingrights.org/data-as-a-tool-for-political-influence-in-the-brazilian-elections/.

Fink, C. (2018). Dangerous speech, Anti-Muslim violence, and Facebook in Myanmar. *Journal of International Affairs. Columbia Sipa.* https://jia.sipa.columbia.edu/dangerous-speech-anti-muslim-violence-and-facebook-myanmar.

George, C., & Venkiteswaran, G. (2019). *Media and power in South East Asia.* Cambridge, UK: Cambridge University Press.

Harsin, J. (2018). Post-truth and critical communication. *Oxford Research Encyclopedias.* https://doi.org/10.1093/acrefore/9780190228613.013.757.

Machado, C., et al. (2018). *News and political information consumption in Brazil: Mapping the first round of the 2018 Brazilian presidential election on Twitter.* Oxford, UK: Project on Computational Propaganda.

Marwick, A., & Lewis, R. (2017). *Media manipulation and disinformation online*. Data and Society Research Institute.

Silverman, C., et al. (2016). Hyperpartisan Facebook pages are publishing false and misleading information at an alarming rate. *Buzzfeed*. https://www.buzzfeed.com/craigsilverman/partisan-fb-pages-analysis?utm_term=.jnB0mGP48x#.toaL7DxX3l.

Vaidhyanathan, S. (2018). *Anti-social media. How Facebook disconnects us and undermines democracy*. Oxford, UK: Oxford University Press.

CHAPTER 6

Conclusions: What Does a Post-truth World Look Like

Abstract This chapter offers some reflections on the media coverage and the on-line conversations around the untimely death of James Le Mesurier, founder of the White Helmets, which epitomizes the post-truth condition as discussed throughout the book. The chapter also presents some closing remarks on the geopolitical significance of the post-truth crisis, by drawing from the multiple case studies presented in the previous chapters. Examples are discussed that show possible avenues of technical, educational, cultural and political intervention that can curb the global spread of misinformation and disinformation, with the broader goal of restoring trust in mediating institutions and in the democratic process.

Keywords Post-truth · Geopolitics · Democracy · Dictatorship · Disinformation · Trust

In the early morning hours of November 11, 2019, James Le Mesurier, founder of Mayday Rescue, a nonprofit organization that trained and supported the White Helmets, was found dead. He had apparently died from the fall from the third-floor ledge of a building where he had his office and home, in the Beyoğlu neighborhood of Istanbul. He was 48 years old. Turkish police investigations didn't suspect foul play and ruled Le Mesurier death as suicide. His wife revealed that Le Mesurier, in the period before his death, had been receiving medical treatment from

© The Author(s) 2020   135
G. Cosentino, *Social Media and the Post-Truth World Order*,
https://doi.org/10.1007/978-3-030-43005-4_6

depression and anxiety. The autopsy and forensic reports corroborated the Turkish police's hypothesis that Le Mesurier had committed suicide.

When the news about Le Mesurier's death broke, speculations and conspiracy theories began to pop up on social media, suggesting multiple scenarios. Some people suspected the involvement of the GRU, the intelligence agency of the Russian Armed Forces, who had allegedly been involved in some recent high-profile assassinations.[1] The suspicion was sparked by a tweet from the official Twitter account of the Ministry of Foreign Affairs of Russia, which just three days before reported the following statement by its Director of the Information and Press Department, Maria Zakharova: "'The White Helmets' co-founder, James Le Mesurier, is a former agent of Britain's MI6, who has been spotted all around the world, including in the #Balkans and the #MiddleEast. His connections to terrorist groups were reported back during his mission in #Kosovo."[2] Many Twitter users took this statement as an indication that, following years of sustained attacks against the White Helmets, the Russian authorities had finally decided to target Le Mesurier directly.

Others, including Syrian President Bashar Al Assad, speaking to Russian television, claimed that Le Mesurier had in fact been killed by Turkish intelligence services working on behalf of the CIA and other Western intelligence agencies.[3] Demonstrating familiarity with the contemporary conspiratorial zeitgeist,[4] Assad linked the death to Le Mesurier to that of Jeffrey Epstein, suggesting that both men knew too many "important secrets" and had "completed their missions" on behalf of Western powers, and as such they had to be eliminated. Assad further speculated that Le

[1] Harding, L. (2018). "Second Skripal poisoning suspect identified as GRU doctor". *The Guardian*. https://www.theguardian.com/uk-news/2018/oct/08/website-names-second-suspect-in-skripal-poisoning-case.

[2] https://twitter.com/mfa_russia/status/1192763676878610432.

[3] Stewart, W., et al. (2019). "Syria's President Assad says British White Helmets founder James Le Mesurier was killed by 'CIA and western intelligence, just like Jeffrey Epstein'". *Mail Online*. https://www.dailymail.co.uk/news/article-7684823/White-Helmets-founder-suicidal-thoughts-claims-wife.html.

[4] The phrase 'Epstein didn't kill himself' has recently become an Internet meme. See Ellis, E. G. (2019). "'Epstein didn't kill himself' and the meme-ing of conspiracy". *Wired*. https://www.wired.com/story/epstein-didnt-kill-himself-conspiracy/.

Mesurier might have been working on a memoir,[5] undesirable for Western powers, where he could have shared a lot of sensitive information about the White Helmets, including, according to the Syrian president, their alleged links to Al-Qaeda and their staging of chemical weapons attacks. A recent hypothesis raised by Turkish newspaper Daily Sabah suggested that Le Mesurier, dubbed in the report as a British 'spy', died while trying to run away from somebody, or that he might have been pushed off the balcony by his own wife.[6]

As expected in these post-truth times, no single, official version established itself as final, not even the one from the Turkish authorities. Around the alternative interpretations of Le Mesurier's death, a heated and polarized debate on social media ensued. Journalists, politicians, academics, activists and trolls that routinely square off on the two sides of the Syrian Civil War, either pro or against the Assad regime, clashed on whether Le Mesurier had been killed by the GRU, by the CIA or had instead killed himself. The discussion on his death inevitably embraced also his legacy as a humanitarian worker. By going through the myriad tweets that poured in the aftermath of his death, one would have been hard-pressed to form an opinion on who James Le Mesurier really was. Was he just a British army veteran and a former employee of the United Nations who later in his life decided to devote himself to the humanitarian assistance of the Syrian civil population affected by the war? This was the image that many of his friends and affiliates, as well long-time reporters on the Syrian conflict,[7] conveyed of him. Le Mesurier had received praises and official recognition for his work with the White Helmets, including being given an OBE award by Queen Elizabeth.

Or was he in fact an MI6 intelligence agent that behind the façade of humanitarian work was actively assisting the pursuit of regime change in

---

[5] RT. (2019). "Assad likens 'suicide' of White Helmets founder to EPSTEIN & other high-profile mystery deaths". *RT*. https://www.rt.com/news/473579-assad-epstein-white-helmets-deaths/.

[6] Ayral, I. (2019) "British 'spy' was likely running away from someone before his death". *Daily Sabah*. https://www.dailysabah.com/investigations/2019/12/10/british-spy-le-mesurier-was-likely-running-away-from-someone-before-his-death.

[7] Di Giovanni, J. (2019). "The brief and inspiring life of James Le Mesurier". *The New York Times*. https://www.nytimes.com/2019/11/14/opinion/syria-white-helmet-founder-dead.html.

Syria, aiding and abetting terrorists, trafficking human organs[8] and helping stage chemical weapons attacks to invite Western military intervention? This is the image of Le Mesurier that pro-Assad social media influencers such as Vanessa Beeley, Russian all news network RT, and count-
less bots and trolls pushed for, before and after his death. The post-truth
fog that engulfed the actions of the White Helmets in Syria reached their
founder all the way to Istanbul, casting multiple shadows on his untimely
death.

Who are we to believe, then? To the accounts of *The New York Times,
The Guardian, The Huffington Post* and other publications who ran eulo-
gies for Le Mesurier after he died, defended his work with the White Helmets, and suggested that depression and stress caused by funding worries
and by a smear campaign had pushed him to suicide? Or to those self-
styled independent publications such as Mint Press, 21st Century Wire,
Global Research, who painted a completely different version of his life
and of the circumstances around his death, implicating him in hideous
crime?

While my initial reaction on Twitter was to suspect Russia's involvement (I also have fallen into the trap of emotional responses on social
media), my own research on the matter led me to support the suicide
hypothesis. The practical and phycological pressures inherent in the management of the White Helmets had taken such a toll on James Le Mesurier
that he could not cope anymore. This explanation for me is coherent with
my personal view and with the information that I have gathered on the
activities of the White Helmets. But having been exposed to conspiratorial material and perspectives throughout the writing process of this book,
there is a part of me that has acquired a knee-jerk tendency to be always
on the lookout for more obscure, convoluted and sinister explanations.
What if Le Mesurier really had a secret agenda? What if the White Helmets really are just a slick PR stunt to cover up Western machinations in
the Middle East? Who can we trust to tell us the truth?

This last question ultimately addresses the fundamental issue at the
core of the post-truth condition, as illustrated and discussed through the
various examples provided in the book. All the case studies examined
showed ruptures and crises in our individual and collective ability to form

---

[8] Bartlett, E. (2018). "UN panel details organ theft, staged attacks by the White Helmets". *Mint Press News.* https://www.mintpressnews.com/un-panel-details-organ-theft-
staged-attacks-white-helmets/253441/.

a substantiated opinion and an evidence-based consensus on a plurality of topics, from vaccines to immigration, from climate change to the war in Syria. We can't reach the truth, not even an approximation of it, because we lack the epistemological conditions to do that. Not because of lack of information, but rather because of the sheer amount of conflicting, misleading and constantly changing information that we are exposed to. Too much information has cluttered our ability to form a rational opinion, and propagandists and demagogues, as discussed by several case studies in this book, know this all too well.

However, the threat of influencers and manipulators, while real, should not be overstated. The epistemic crisis predates their actions, and it is structurally linked to very conditions of our contemporary democratic societies. As argued throughout the book, the authorities that have helped us structure our social and political reality in the second half of the twentieth century—scientific institutions, public institutions, the media, political parties—can't rely anymore on the trust that allows them to aggregate the public opinion around a consensual view of objective reality. As Harsin, D'Ancona, McIntyre and others rightly point, post-truth ultimately rests on a crisis of trust: citizens don't trust institutions anymore. The social bond had been broken. Social media, alternative information outlets, Internet subcultures, tribal aggregations, political influencers and information warfare outfits have carved spaces of dissent, suspicious and disbeliefs large enough to question the authority of established political and cultural organizations. Conspiracy theories, fake news and rumor bombs fill the void created by such ruptures, with simplistic, paranoid interpretations overriding more complex or thorough inquiries of reality built on sound theoretical models and empirical methods. As trust in journalism and scientific inquiry declines, so does our support for democracy, its processes and its institutions. Ultimately, in an almost predictable yet no less unsettling Orwellian drift, the very foundations of objective reality begin to shake.

As discussed by the various case studies provided, the epistemic crisis suffered by Western media and democracy can be fully grasped only if projected on a more global scale. The backdrop is the broader crisis of the so-called Western 'modernity package', based on liberal democracy, multiculturalism, secularism and free market capitalism. The last grand narrative of the twentieth century can't present itself anymore as an authoritative perspective on world affairs for the twenty-first century. The Western globalist, centrist and technocratic view of the world is rejected from the left and from the right of the global public opinion, and it is crumbling under such concerted assault. Western ethnonationalists and hostile State actors jointly cooperate to undermine its geopolitical standing. In the interregnum between the decline of the Western—and especially Anglo-American—global hegemony and a future, yet-to-be-seen world order, the truth and its ideological, political and cultural foundations crumble. A regime of truth, in Foucauldian terms, is dying.

So, the answer to the questions above is that we won't be able to know the truth about the death of James Le Mesurier, at least for now. We might have our own individual interpretation of it, but there won't be a single, agreed-upon version of the event, nor of the man's legacy. We can't know the truth because we can't trust anybody with enough authority on their methods, motives and objective to establish the truth for us. We lack the cultural and political conditions that can underpin our belief systems, structure our relation and interpretation of objective reality and bridge our ideological divisions. Social media platforms, by allowing sensational, polarizing and misleading content to overshadow more cautious, objective and lucid discussions, by creating a hypercompetitive attention economy that rewards virality over veracity and by skirting their responsibility as carriers of problematic or dangerous content, are further contributing to the erosion of rational and democratic public discussion and consensual political reality. This critical techno-political conjuncture plays out both in the Western world and in various countries around the globe, where post-truth has become a battlefield for the conflicts that are ensuing around the crisis of the Western hegemony. Russia and China of course are the most serious contenders in this global battle to redefine power relations and to establish new hegemonic conditions.

So, is this what a post-truth world looks like? Should one just give up, once and for all, on the idea that objective truth exists, and that through sound inquiry, research and free dialectic exchange we can aspire to reach it? Are we condemned to be subjugated by social actors, whether State institutions or rogue entities, who will employ the most sophisticated and effective forms of public opinion manipulation, including the use of the latest technologies, such as deepfakes?[9] This book is a testimony to the fact that post-truth presents a clear, present and widespread danger.

---

[9] Schwartz, O. (2018). "You thought fake news was bad? Deep fakes are where truth goes to die". *The Guardian.* https://www.theguardian.com/technology/2018/nov/12/deep-fakes-fake-news-truth?CMP=Share_iOSApp_Other#img-1.

A report by researchers at Oxford University revealed that 70 countries around the world were affected by social media manipulation campaigns in 2019,[10] proving that post-truth politics via social media is indeed a growing global phenomenon. As prominent global actors shift their interests to resource-rich regions such as Africa, an intensification of information warfare is bound to affect this continent as well, as already testified by academic and journalistic investigations.[11] The global dynamics of disinformation are bound to become even more pervasive and disruptive.

There are, however, silver linings in this gloomy scenario. Grassroots, open-source journalistic investigation efforts such as that provided by Bellingcat, while still struggling to gain widespread legitimacy, are nonetheless providing collaborative, evidence-based and effective real-time verification of events that might otherwise become clouded by the same midst of uncertainty, confusion and spin that has bewildered thousands of citizens in many occasions before. Social media platforms are becoming more receptive to the warnings and pleas made by activists, NGOs, journalists and scholars on their potentially disastrous effects in world regions characterized by volatile political conditions and fragile democratic institutions. While not fully acknowledging their responsibility as content platforms and not simply technology platforms—as Sacha Baron Cohen lamented—Facebook, Twitter and YouTube have, however, become more aware that the powerful tools they give their users can become instrumental to campaigns of hate, harassment and radicalization. The algorithmic amplification of potentially incendiary content is now more closely monitored by social media platforms. Facebook has set up a 'war room' to monitor and curb the effects of disinformation on elections worldwide, so that to prevent the influence campaign that interfered with the 2016 US elections and

---

[10] Bradshaw, S., & Howard, P. (2019). *The global disinformation order: 2019 global inventory of organised—Social media manipulation.* Oxford, UK: Oxford Internet Institute.

[11] Grossman, S., et al. (2019). "Evidence of Russia-linked influence operations in Africa". *Stanford Internet Observatory.* https://fsi-live.s3.us-west-1.amazonaws.com/s3fs-public/29oct2019_sio_russia_linked_influence_operations_in_africa.final_pdf; Alba, D., & Frenkel, S. (2019). "Russia tests new disinformation tactics in Africa to expand influence". *The New York Times.* https://www.nytimes.com/2019/10/30/technology/russia-facebook-disinformation-africa.html.

with the Brexit referendum from happening again.[12] Twitter has decided to ban all political advertisements.[13]

These are all laudable initiatives that demonstrate a collective reaction against what might otherwise be an irreversible drift toward a post-truth era. There is, however, only so much that Bellingcat can do to counter the manipulative tactics of dozens of malicious actors worldwide. Technology companies, furthermore, can't be expected to provide a solution for a problem so complex and pervasive as the one described throughout the book. They definitely can and should be held accountable, monitored and sanctioned, but they ultimately are private corporations that respond to their shareholders before anybody else. Educational initiatives can have longer-lasting effects, and institutions have a prominent responsibility in educating children, students and citizens on the dangers associated with misinformation and disinformation. Media literacy programs have been launched in a plurality of countries, with some examples, like that of Finland, standing out for its sharp focus on the threats posed by social media manipulations by foreign agents.[14] Governments can also learn to better defend themselves from influence campaigns, and success stories, like that of France's comprehensive response to the 2017 cyberattacks against Macron,[15] indicate that effective countermeasures can be put in place against the spreading of malicious content.

However, for democracies to really overcome the post-truth predicament, the more structural and profound work needs to be at a cultural and political level, with the main goal of reestablishing trust among citizens, and between citizens and institutions. As theorized and extensively discussed by the various examples provided, a crisis of truth is first and foremost a crisis of trust, signaling a sociopolitical breakdown even before

[12] Frenkel, S., & Isaac, M. (2018). "Inside Facebook's election 'war room'". *The New York Times*. https://www.nytimes.com/2018/09/19/technology/facebook-election-war-room.html.

[13] BBC News. (2019). "Twitter to ban all political advertising". *BBC News*. https://www.bbc.com/news/world-us-canada-50243306.

[14] Mackinstosh, E. (2019). "Finland is winning the war on fake news. What it's learned may be crucial to Western democracy". *CNN*. https://edition.cnn.com/interactive/2019/05/europe/finland-fake-news-intl/.

[15] Schmidt, C. (2018). "How France beat back information manipulation (and how other democracies might do the same)". *NiemanLab*. https://www.niemanlab.org/2018/09/how-france-beat-back-information-manipulation-and-how-other-democracies-might-do-the-same/.

an epistemic one. Bonds of trust will need to be re-established in order to create the conditions for truth to be again assessed, arbitered and commonly shared. This might be an even harder task that simply addressing a post-truth crisis, because it leads to questions that cut at the very foundations of our common living. Do we trust that our collective choices and actions are for the greatest welfare of our society? Do we trust the politicians, scientists and businessman to which we mandate the leadership of our communities? Do we trust ourselves, as citizens, as having the best interests of our society and of the planet at heart, and not simply our individual needs and desires? If post-truth really signals the demise of the neoliberal order with American democracy and consumer capitalism at its helm, as argued in this book, then it means people have stopped trusting such a political economy model. If democracies, both in the West and in the Global South, are to survive the growing challenges posed by autocracies and dictatorships, they will need to radically work on restoring trust within their body politic. As threats of world conflicts and environmental catastrophes loom large, we can't afford to be blindsided by post-truth. The Western democratic model needs to regain the trust of people around the world, by presenting itself as a viable and reliable model of multiculturalism, socioeconomic justice and environmental sustainability for the twenty-first century. Then maybe citizens will begin to trust again, and the truth will have more solid grounds to stand on.

Index

Manufactured by Amazon.ca
Bolton, ON

45128597R00087